DAD : CAROLYN
HAVE A WONDERFUL
XMAS —
I LOVE YOU BOTH
Mom

Xmas 1985
Dear Micheal & Caroline —
Here is something to motivate you
for your next cultural trip.
Best Wishes for the New Year!
Love Briany.

This book was made possible by:

 American Express International, Inc.

 Kodak Japan K. K.

 JAPAN AIR LINES

Tokyo Hilton International

Apple Computer, Inc.

OLYMPUS CAMERAS

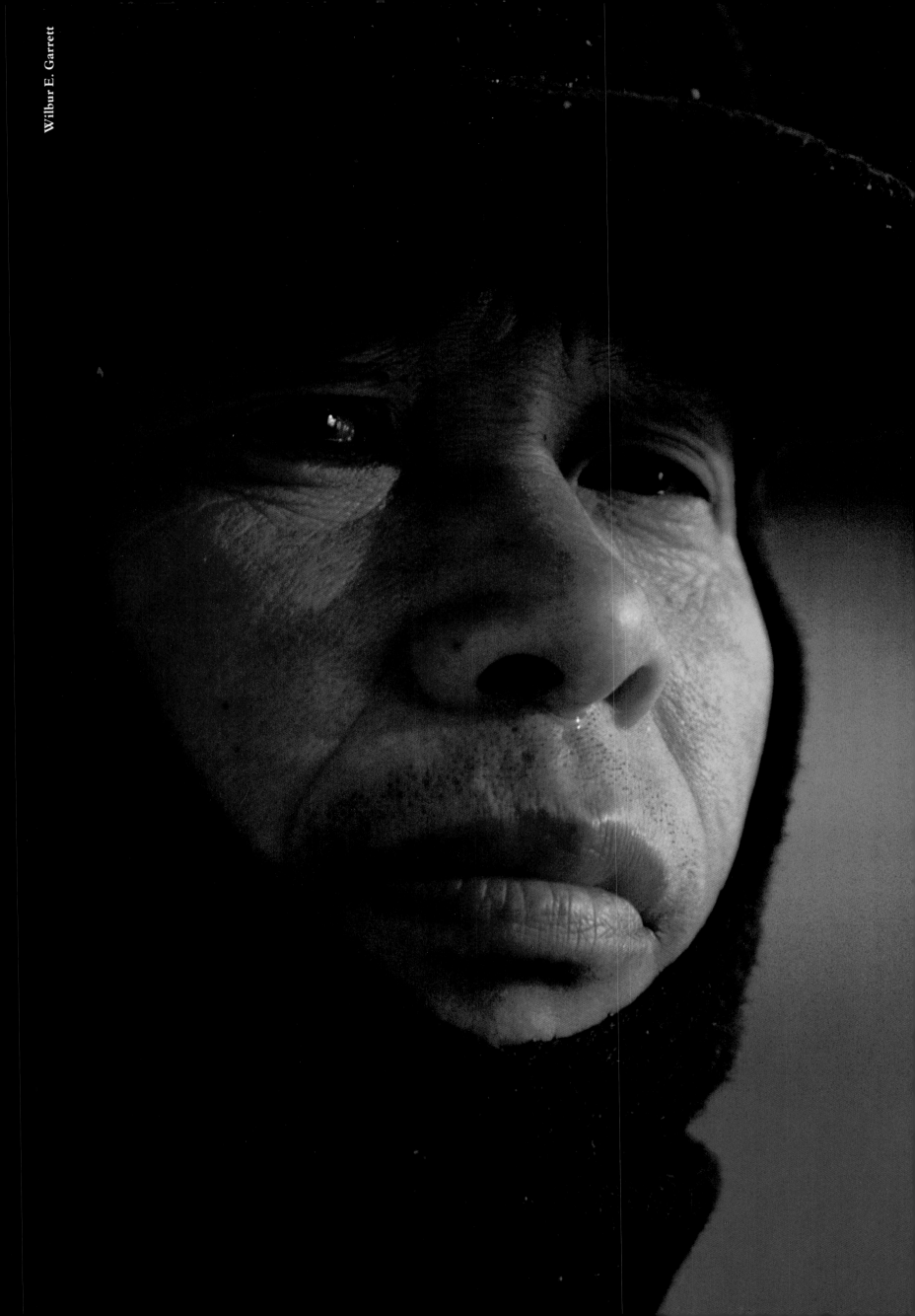

When *A Day in the Life of Japan* was first discussed, people reacted in many different ways. Some told us the idea was absurd. They said that pictures taken on just one day couldn't say anything new or significant about a country as ancient and complex as Japan. Others doubted that the Japanese business community would ever support such a far-fetched idea. And many warned us that no matter how good the pictures were, the public just might not be interested.

The only explanation of how this book came into existence is that we were lucky. We were lucky when we were able to find generous sponsors. We were lucky that June 7th, the day of the shoot, missed the start of the rainy season by one day. (It poured all over Japan for the week following the shoot day.) We were lucky when International Christian University assigned their graduating class of translators to work on the project as their final class assignment. We were lucky that so many people were willing to offer us their contacts and stake their reputations—something not done lightly in Japan—on the performance of our photographers. We were lucky because so many individuals contributed their time, their knowledge of Japan and their enthusiasm to turn this crazy idea into a reality. But most of all we were lucky that the Japanese people allowed the photographers to see a Japan which is rarely shown to foreigners.

We are grateful to the photographers who devoted their skills with such dedication . . . to the business community which contributed so generously . . . and above all to the people of Japan, without whose kindness and warmth this project would not have been possible.

Graeme Outerbridge

First published 1985 by
William Collins Sons & Co.
Ltd., Toronto, New York,
London, Glasgow, Sydney,
Auckland, Johannesburg.

Canadian Cataloguing in
Publication Data
Main entry under title:
A Day in the Life of Japan

ISBN 0-00-217580-0

1. Japan-description and
travel-1945-Views.
I. Smolan, Rick.
II. Cohen, David.

DS811.D39 1985
915.2'002'2   C85-099462-4

Project Directors
Rick Smolan and David Cohen

Art Director
Leslie Smolan

Cover photograph shot on
Ektachrome film by Jodi Cobb

Printed in Japan
First printing September 1985

10 9 8 7 6 5 4 3 2 1

A Day in the Life of Japan

Photographed by 100 of the
world's leading photojournalists
on one day, June 7, 1985

Collins Publishers

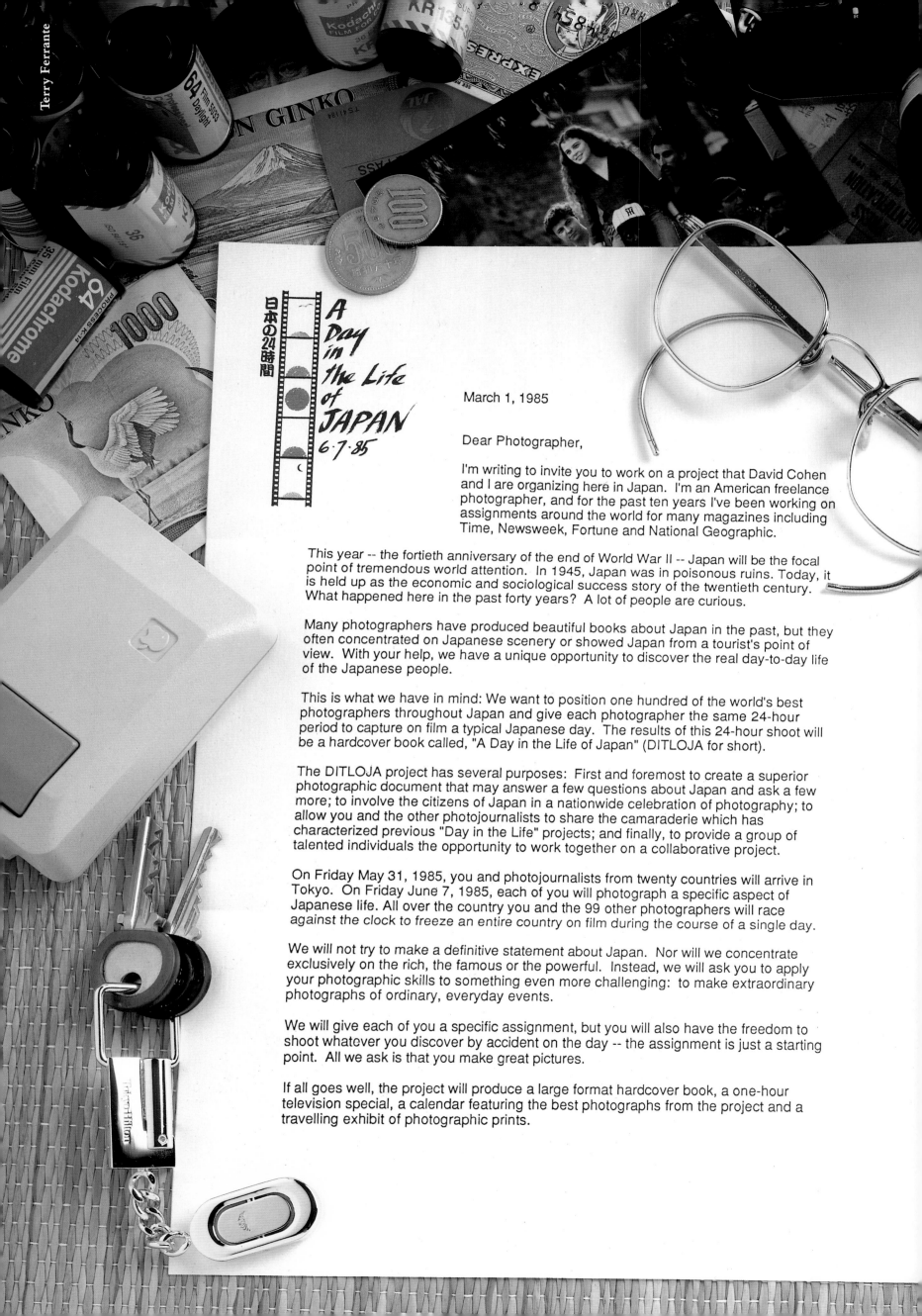

日本の24時間 **A Day in the Life of JAPAN** 6·7·85

March 1, 1985

Dear Photographer,

I'm writing to invite you to work on a project that David Cohen and I are organizing here in Japan. I'm an American freelance photographer, and for the past ten years I've been working on assignments around the world for many magazines including Time, Newsweek, Fortune and National Geographic.

This year -- the fortieth anniversary of the end of World War II -- Japan will be the focal point of tremendous world attention. In 1945, Japan was in poisonous ruins. Today, it is held up as the economic and sociological success story of the twentieth century. What happened here in the past forty years? A lot of people are curious.

Many photographers have produced beautiful books about Japan in the past, but they often concentrated on Japanese scenery or showed Japan from a tourist's point of view. With your help, we have a unique opportunity to discover the real day-to-day life of the Japanese people.

This is what we have in mind: We want to position one hundred of the world's best photographers throughout Japan and give each photographer the same 24-hour period to capture on film a typical Japanese day. The results of this 24-hour shoot will be a hardcover book called, "A Day in the Life of Japan" (DITLOJA for short).

The DITLOJA project has several purposes: First and foremost to create a superior photographic document that may answer a few questions about Japan and ask a few more; to involve the citizens of Japan in a nationwide celebration of photography; to allow you and the other photojournalists to share the camaraderie which has characterized previous "Day in the Life" projects; and finally, to provide a group of talented individuals the opportunity to work together on a collaborative project.

On Friday May 31, 1985, you and photojournalists from twenty countries will arrive in Tokyo. On Friday June 7, 1985, each of you will photograph a specific aspect of Japanese life. All over the country you and the 99 other photographers will race against the clock to freeze an entire country on film during the course of a single day.

We will not try to make a definitive statement about Japan. Nor will we concentrate exclusively on the rich, the famous or the powerful. Instead, we will ask you to apply your photographic skills to something even more challenging: to make extraordinary photographs of ordinary, everyday events.

We will give each of you a specific assignment, but you will also have the freedom to shoot whatever you discover by accident on the day -- the assignment is just a starting point. All we ask is that you make great pictures.

If all goes well, the project will produce a large format hardcover book, a one-hour television special, a calendar featuring the best photographs from the project and a travelling exhibit of photographic prints.

Although this project is supported by the Prime Minister of Japan, The Foreign Ministry and the Japanese External Trade Organization (JETRO), as well as by American Express and a number of other private companies, it is not a public relations exercise or a tourist promotion. Everyone supporting this project understands that you are a journalist and that they will have no editorial control over what you shoot or what is selected for the book. DITLOJA will be an honest look at Japan, not just another book of pretty picture postcards.

By the same token, there is no guarantee that every photographer will get a picture in the book. That depends on whether or not you have a good day on June 7th.

At the moment, the twenty of us on staff are frantically putting the last pieces in place to make sure everything goes smoothly when you and the other photographers arrive. If working with us on this crazy idea appeals to you, here are a few things you will need to know and a few things we need from you very quickly:

1) **Biography:** Don't be modest. We need as much information as possible about your photography career -- awards, exhibits, books published, etc.

2) **Film:** Kodak Japan will supply you with 30 rolls of film (Kodachrome, Ektachrome or Tri-X). It would help us to know your film requirements in advance.

3) **Ground Transportation:** If your assignment requires it, you will be provided with a free rental car courtesy of Nissan Motors.

4) **Translators:** We have made special arrangements for members of the graduating class of translators from International Christian University to assist DITLOJA photographers as their graduation project.

5) **Roommates:** If you take advantage of the hotel rooms provided to you courtesy of the Tokyo Hilton International during your stay in Tokyo, you will share a twin room with a famous photographer at absolutely no extra charge.

6) **Payment:** All expenses including air and ground travel will be covered by us. In return for the one day of shooting you have the choice of receiving either an honorarium of $750 or an Apple 512K Macintosh computer system and Imagewriter printer. Olympus cameras will also supply one of their new auto-focus AFLS 35mm cameras to each participant.

There is no question that this will be the most challenging of all the projects we've attempted to date. DITLOJA will be the first time that we have tried the "Day in the Life" concept in a non-western, non-English speaking country. We need people of your calibre and experience to ensure that this book will be as succesful as our first three "Day in the Life" books.

We hope you will be able to lend your skills, and believe you will be as fascinated with Japan as we are.

Best regards,

Rick Smolan

Statistics bear out what nearly any visitor to Japan notices: the Japanese eat a lot of fish. With little more than 2 percent of the world's population, Japan consumes nearly 15 percent of the world's catch. Per capita, they eat 8 times more fish and shellfish than Americans do and 15 times more than the Chinese. Japanese-registered boats (many of which have never been to Japan) fish in every ocean of the world, in the Arctic Sea and off Antarctica. In skill, volume and value, Japan is easily the world's foremost fishing nation.

Japanese eat their fish stewed, salted, smoked, broiled, baked and, of course, raw in *sushi* and as *sashimi*. Fish eating comes easy in Japan. No place in the country is more than 100 kilometers (60 miles) from the sea, and few Japanese live further than a short walk from several fish-shops (which are more numerous than outlets for meat or poultry). Nature, unkind to Japan in many things, has been lavish with fish: the warm *kuroshio* and cold *oyashio* currents meet off Japan's Pacific coast and still provide some of the richest fishing grounds in the world (although there has been over-fishing in recent years). The Buddhist prohibition against killing animals for food and the shortage of grazing land also helped, historically, to confirm the Japanese as fish-eaters. It's good for them, too. The Japanese now have the longest life expectancy in the world, often attributed in part to their low-fat diet.

In 1985 there were 447,000 Japanese fishermen going to sea in home waters and around the world, down 7 percent from 1978. The Japanese fisherman continued to be rightly admired for his toughness and skill, much as the cowboy is idolized by beef-eating Americans. (Japan even has "dude fishing boats," just as the United States has dude ranches.) Offered the choice of steak or prime seafood, many Japanese will choose the latter, and this is likely to continue as long as there are fish left in the sea.

●*Below, top*

After the fish have been inspected and marked, the auctioneers take over. Each has developed his own trademark repertoire of calls and gestures.

Photographer:
David Burnett

●*Right*

"Tuna hell" at Tsukiji fish market.

Photographer:
Bruno Barbey

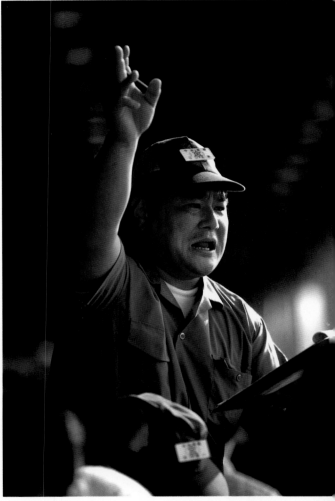

●*Previous page*

Frozen tuna arrive by truck at the Tsukiji central fish market, a maze of cavernous buildings in the heart of Tokyo. Basic to *sushi,* tuna is the most popular fish in Japan, and supplies come from all over the world. On June 7, 1985, the best cuts of tuna were retailing at ¥ 5,000 (US $20) a pound and up.

Photographer:
David Burnett

●*Above*

At 4:30 AM on June 7, as the sun rises over the Sumida River, a worker at the Tsukiji fish market axes the tails from the carcasses of frozen tuna. Tsukiji was built near the original site of Edo, the small fishing village that became Tokyo.

Photographer:
David Burnett

●*Right, middle and bottom*

Buying agents for fish retailers, restaurateurs and *sushi* chefs bid on individual tuna carcasses after inspecting small samples of meat. The fish are turned over with a hook-like implement so that all sides can be studied.

Photographer:
David Burnett

The bullet—one of the world's most famous trains. A long and narrow country, Japan is ideal for high-speed rail travel. The first bullet train reached 200 kilometers (120 miles) per hour on July 1, 1964, just in time for the Tokyo Olympic Games. It reduced travel time between Tokyo and Osaka from 6 hours 30 minutes to 3 hours 10 minutes and cost ¥ 380 billion (US$1.2 billion) to build. Since then, the system has been greatly extended and has carried more than three billion people the equivalent of 30,000 trips around the earth without a single passenger fatality. The unique safety record comes from sound design and maintenance. Every pair of wheels on the train has a motor and disk brakes, and the entire track is checked every ten days for signs of wear. The trains stop automatically during earthquakes.

Japanese call the train not "bullet," a term used only by foreigners, but *Shinkansen*, which means "New Trunk Line." Individual trains have poetic names like *Light* and *Echo*. All have restaurants or buffet-bars, some have shops, but none have sleepers (not necessary). The ride is supremely comfortable, but the unreserved sections get as crowded as all Japanese trains.

Yoshio Yamada has achieved what, according to the surveys, most of today's Japanese want—a steady, lifelong job with a big company. Yamada is a *kacho*, or section chief, of the Second Grain Department of Nissho Iwai, a major Tokyo trading company. This makes him a *sarariman*, which comes from the English words "salary man" and once simply meant a worker who was paid by the month.

The *sarariman* is normally a white-collar worker. In principle, he stays with his company or

government department for life. Job-hopping by ambitious Japanese is frowned on, and all but unknown.

The *sarariman* can normally expect automatic advancement in salary and title as his job and family responsibilities grow. (His ceiling will basically depend on his education.) He will receive company housing or a low-interest loan, company medical care, job security, regular bonuses and a one-time retirement bonus of several years' salary.

In return, he is expected to be loyal, to put the company's interests ahead of his own (or, more precisely, to find satisfaction in being a good company man), to work without watching the clock, to be agreeable to colleagues and respectful to superiors and to take few vacations or none at all. The *sarariman's* wife—and most Japanese parents hope their daughters will marry a *sarariman*—should be prepared to take second position to his job, to get him to work on time spotlessly turned out in his sober business suit, and to endure without complaint the many nights he will bring his work home or be out drinking with clients and workmates—all in the line of duty.

The *sarariman* lifestyle has been widely criticized, even in Japan, for its conformity, its narrow horizons, the strain it puts on families and marriages, its loneliness and lack of real friendships outside of working hours. There is truth in these charges. But the system has also given Japan what many people think is the most diligent, conscientious, best-educated middle management in the world.

● *Previous page and left*

Yoshio Yamada's wife gets him off to work. He wears *suteteko*, extra-long cotton underpants favored by Japanese men in summer. The average *sarariman* commutes an hour and a half a day, each way. His home is modest, his workplace palatial—the standard Japanese order of priority. Business meetings take place all day, usually in a corner of a crowded, busy department. Private offices are rare.

● *Above*

Kiyoharu Kodama, 44, of Rishiri Island off northern Hokkaido has been a fisherman all of his working life, as was his father before him. In 1945, his father reached Rishiri after escaping from Soviet internment on Sakhalin Island. Remote steering on Kodama's boat enables him to catch octopus single-handedly.
Photographer:
Wilbur E. Garrett

● *Right*

In Nemuro, eastern Hokkaido —the Japanese city nearest to Soviet-held territory—fishermen's wives clean nets.
Photographer:
Jennifer Erwitt

● *Far right*

Boiling octopus on Rishiri Island.
Photographer:
Wilbur E. Garrett

● *Above*

Temple windows in Yubari,
Hokkaido.
Photographer:
Steve Krongard

● *Right*

Off to school at a Hokkaido
ranch.
Photographer:
David Alan Harvey

8:00 AM

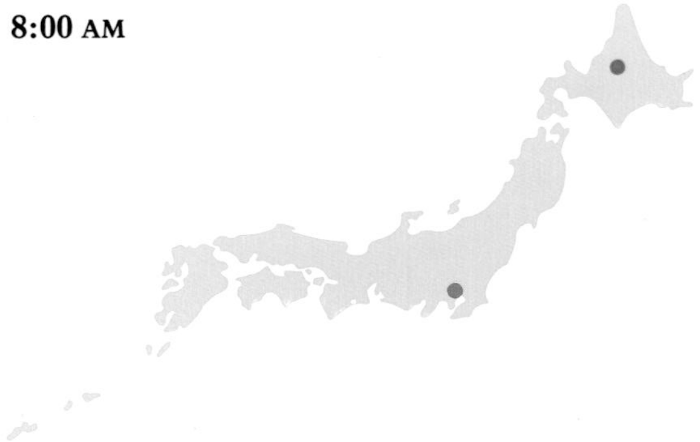

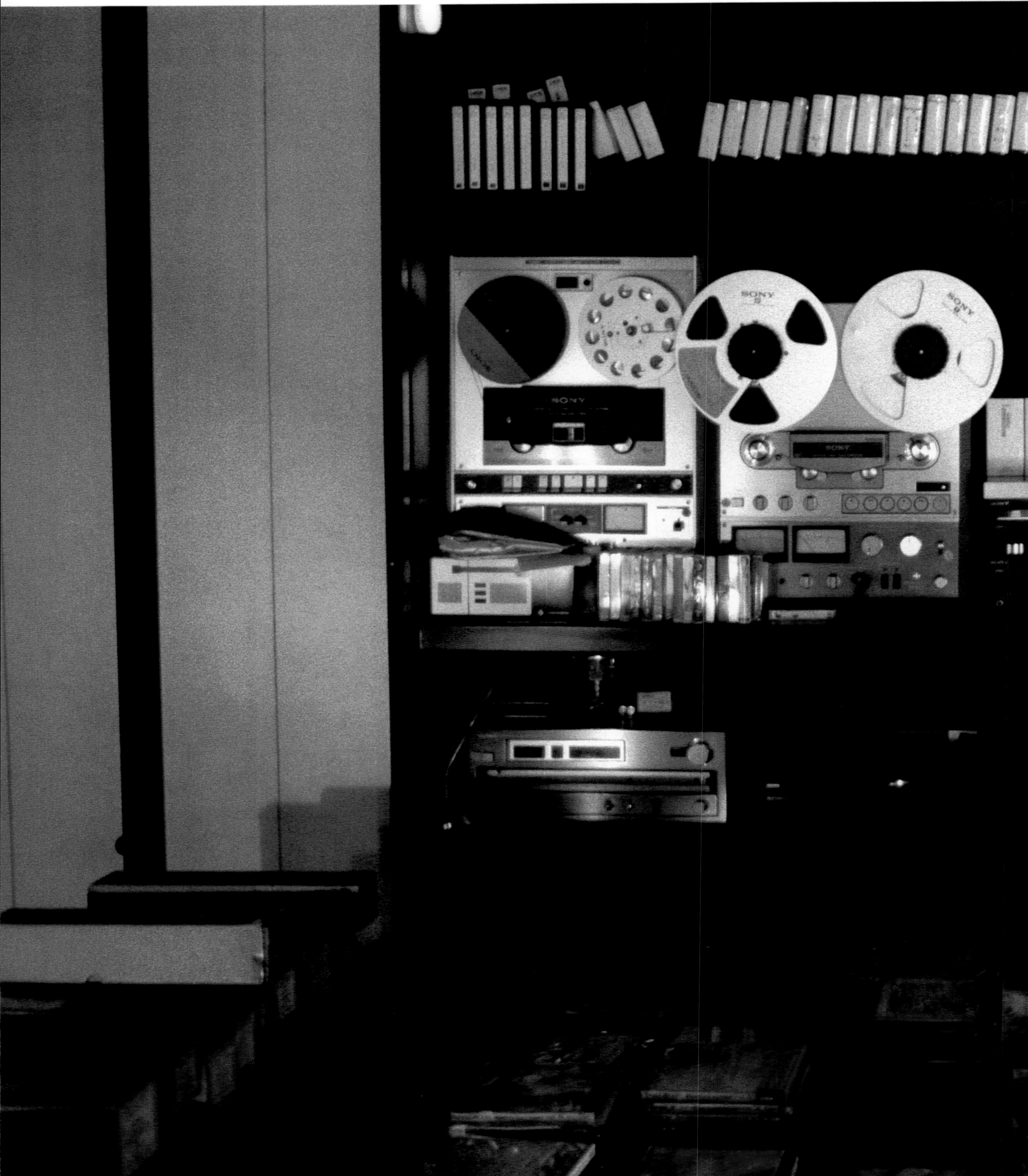

After breakfast at their Hok-kaido ranch, Hiroshi Hamaguchi and his wife are absorbed in a popular Japanese *homu dorama* (home drama) called *Miotsukushi,* a salty tale about a romance between a handsome young fisherman and a soy sauce heiress who someday hope to make beautiful sushi together.

Photographer:
David Alan Harvey

● *Left*

National Geographic photographer Rich Clarkson spent June 7th with Akio Morita, Chairman of Sony Corporation.

"I got to Morita's house early and was prepared to wait outside until he left for work but Mrs. Morita surprised me by inviting me in for a cup of coffee. Mr. Morita showed up a minute later wearing a pair of Levi's, and he took me into a living room filled with every Sony gadget imaginable. There were dozens of speakers along the walls, and on top of the piano was every compact digital disc ever made. He asked me if I liked music and I said 'of course.'

"He looked at me, smiled and put a disc into the player and hit the button. I looked around the room to see which of all the speakers the music was going to come out of. At first it was very quiet and I had to strain to figure out what the music was. Then I recognized it—the theme from the movie *2001.* The melody seemed to be coming from everywhere, but suddenly it broke into a crescendo of sound and the whole room filled with music unlike anything I'd ever heard before. If any of the neighbors were still asleep before that, they weren't any longer.

"I was just stunned by the whole thing and he smiled at me, stopped the disc and said, 'Now I will show you my secret.' He pointed up and there were these huge twin woofers built into the ceiling, eight feet across. We were actually standing inside this huge speaker disguised as a living room. It was the damnedest thing I'd ever seen!"

Photographer:
Rich Clarkson

● *Below*

Kiyoshi Kikkawa, 74, is visited by his wife at the Hiroshima Hospital for Atomic Bomb Survivors. Kikkawa, who was severely burned by the bomb, calls himself "Atomic Bomb Victim #1." He formerly ran an atomic bomb souvenir shop where he posed for tourist snapshots. Kikkawa is in the hospital because he recently suffered a stroke.

Photographer:
Eikoh Hosoe

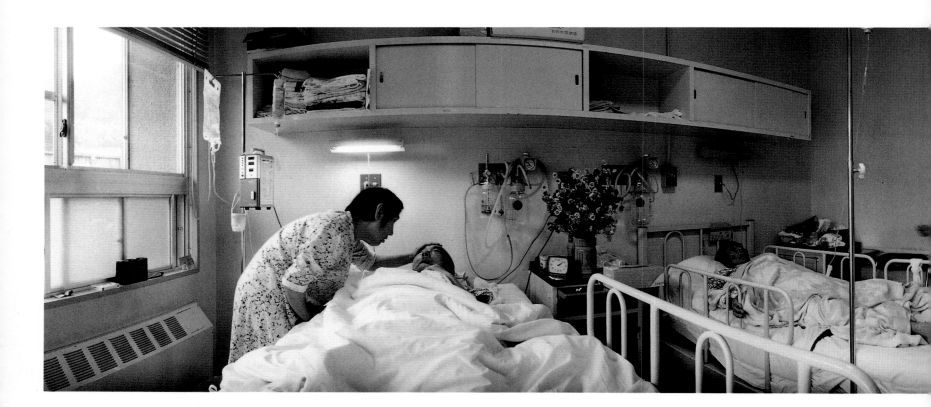

● *Previous pages 38–39*

Burning straw from the last crop in Nishiune, Okayama Prefecture.

Photographer:
Anne Day

● *Previous page*

Commuters from the outer suburbs head for Tokyo.

Photographer:
Jay Maisel

● *Above*

Atomic bomb survivors do morning exercises at the hospital.

Photographer:
Eikoh Hosoe

● *Right*

With the world's longest life expectancy, the population of Japan is rapidly aging. By the year 2020, nearly one-quarter of all Japanese will be over 65. Although age is traditionally respected in Japan, the needs of senior citizens are already straining the limited social security system. Eighty percent of the elderly live with their families. This couple is in a home for the aged in Hachioji, a Tokyo suburb.

Photographer:
Junichi Tanabe

● *Left, top*

High-school students travel by train. They get special discount fares on the Japanese National Railways (JNR).

Photographer:
Misha Erwitt

● *Left, middle*

A JNR *oshiya* or "pusher-in" resolves a Japanese etiquette problem: the passenger is determined to get to work on time, but the train doors cannot close unless he gets in or out. The other passengers are too polite to interfere, so the *oshiya*, in courteous white gloves, helps him decide. In the winter, commuters wear more clothes, and the JNR employs extra pushers-in.

Photographer:
Andrew Stawicki

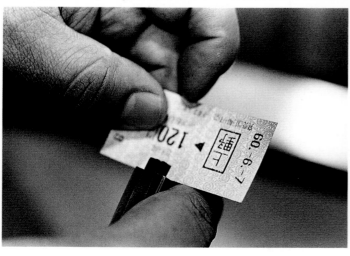

120-yen (45-cent) train
ket issued at Ueno Station
Tokyo on June 7, 1985. The
panese date shows the six-
h year of the reign of
peror Hirohito. This ticket
ll take you three or four
ps on the JNR urban
tem.

tographer:

ku Kurita

● *Below*

Shinjuku Station, Tokyo, the
busiest train station in the
world. The Japanese call the
rush hour *tsukin jigoku* or
"commuter hell." Japanese
commuter trains, many owned
by the same companies that
own the department stores,
are fast, immaculately clean,
punctual and often brutally
overcrowded. Injuries sometimes occur when passengers

jammed together fall down
like dominoes when the train
stops. Old people and parents
with young children in tow
stay off the trains during rush
hour, but the system efficiently
and uncomfortably carries 19
million passengers a day on
28,000 trains.

Photographer:

Tadanori Saito

● *Following page*

Every morning at 8:30, the
staff of the Asahikawa Coca-
Cola bottling plant exercise for
ten minutes. Introduced dur-
ing the American occupation,
Coke competes with popular
Japanese soft drinks such as
Pocari Sweat and Calpis.

Photographer:

Diego Goldberg

● *Above*

A bag lady in a smart Tokyo
shopping district. Like all big
cities, Tokyo has its share of
street people.
Photographer:
Bruno Barbey

● *Above*

A department-store section
manager gives employees their
morning pep talk before the

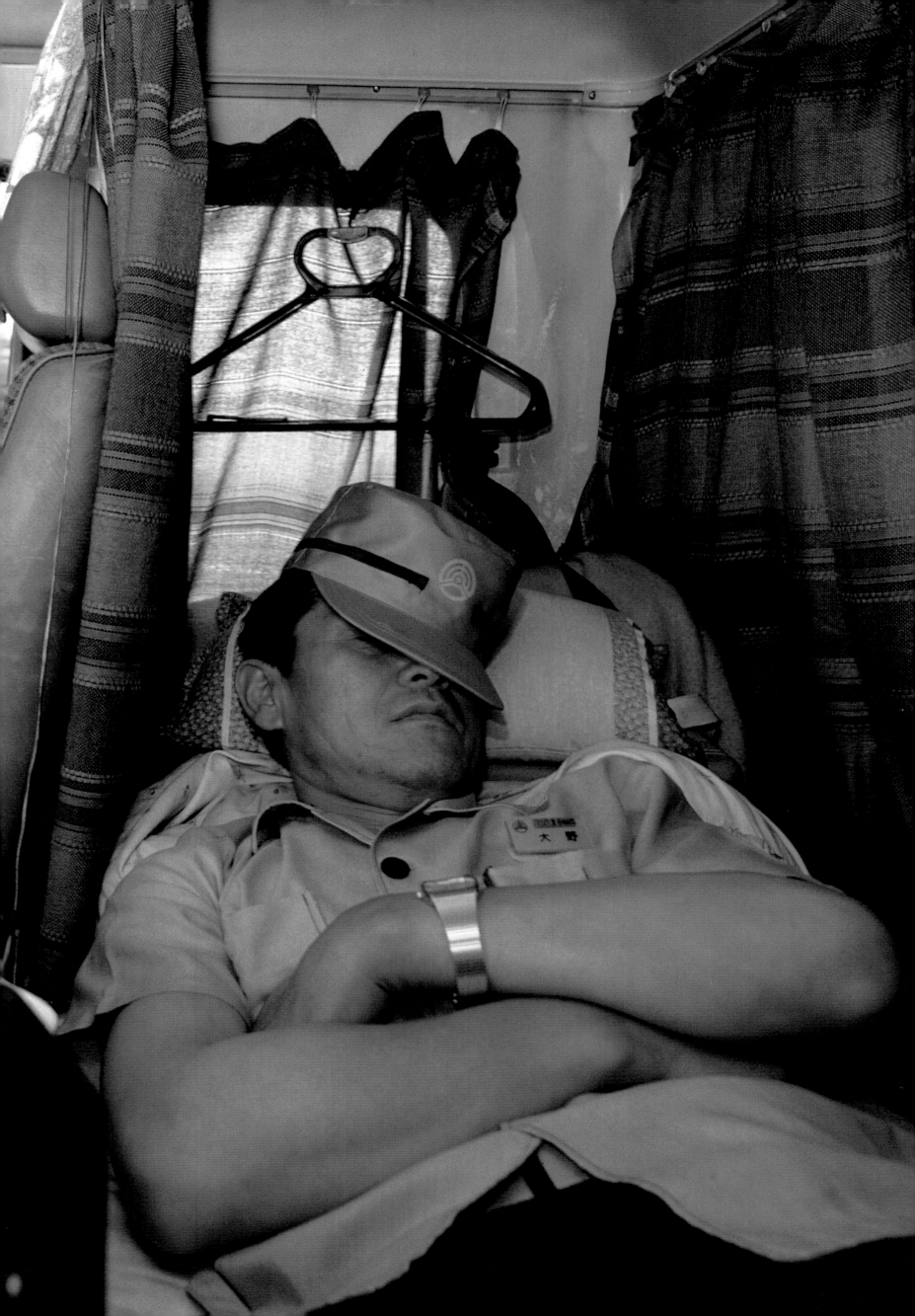

James Nachtwey

Andy Levin

eft

neeting of a Nissan
rkers' quality-control circle.
e system, aimed at reducing
ects to zero, originated in
United States. The
anese have improved it.
ographer:
dy Levin

● *Below*

Outside a trendy clothing
store in Hokkaido.
Photographer:
Diego Goldberg

revious page

san automobile assembly
at the Murayama plant
Tokyo. The worker
lerneath the car has one of
toughest jobs on the line
ause he works with his
ds above his head all day.
Detroit, this job is often
en to the most junior
ployees. In Japan, the job
ught after because it is
sidered important and leads
romotion.
ographer:
dy Levin

● *Previous pages 50–51*

An expert from Tokyo in-
structs agricultural workers in
Tohno, Iwate Prefecture,
about picking and packing lettuce. For many years Iwate
was famous for rice, but recent
rice surpluses have caused the
Ministry of Agriculture to en-
courage the planting of new
crops. Lettuce is a relative
newcomer to the Japanese
scene.
Photographer:
Ian Lloyd

● *Previous pages 52–53*

Toshiro Ohno and Takao
Morioka of Shikoku Seino
Trucking Company on a
22-hour run from Matsuyama
on Shikoku Island to Tokyo.
Torakkuyaro, or long-distance
truck drivers, have become
minor Japanese folk heroes.
Photographer:
Dan Dry

● *Previous pages 54–55*

Japan has by far the lowest
crime rate in the industrial
world. (There is, for example,
one robbery in Japan for every
244 in the United States.) It
also has the most visible
policemen, called in Japanese
omawari-san or literally
"Respected Mr. Walking-
Around." Most city blocks
have tiny police boxes where
vigilant officers watch the
street and politely keep track
of people's comings and go-
ings. For years, Japan has also

maintained an army of realistic
life-size fiberglass models of
policemen who stand by the
side of the road or sit in stationary patrol cars. The latest
trend in police vigilance is the
life-size photograph, keeping
watch on a speed-limit zone
east of the Susa tunnel on the
Sanin Coast.
Photographer:
James Nachtwey

● *Right*

Takehiko Iwase pauses out Akihabara Station before delivering this brand new 71-kilogram (157-pound) refrigerator.

Photographer:
Neal Ulevich

● *Above*

Japan is the electronics capital of the world, and Tokyo's Akihabara district is the discount electronics capital of Japan. Akihabara's streets and alleys are jammed with electronics shops of all sizes and specialties. On June 7, 1985, visitors to Akihabara were already buying the latest electronic gadgets of 1986.

Bunzo Miyazawa, 48, masquerades as a spaceman among his wares. Along with the Walkmans and microphones on display, he sells a variety of bigger items such as refrigerators and televisions. Mr. Miyazawa says, "I sell everything but electric chairs." (Japanese are hanged.)

Photographer:
Neal Ulevich

● *Right*

Akihabara, June 7, 1985. Watches with hands have gone out of style.

Photographer:
Neal Ulevich

● *Left*

At 10 AM, receptionists at Mitsukoshi in Tokyo greet the first customers of the day. The oldest department store in the world, Mitsukoshi first opened its doors in 1673. These young ladies also answer questions, operate the elevators and wipe escalator handrails.

Photographer:
Gerd Ludwig

● *Above, top*

Samples of the season's new green tea are prepared in the main Mitsukoshi store in Nihonbashi, Tokyo. On June 7, 1985, the Japanese tea harvest was already well under way.

Photographer:
Gerd Ludwig

● *Above*

"I happened to be in Takamatsu, Shikoku, on a once-a-year company trip. I walked around alone, as usual, trying to capture the town with my camera. Since June 7 was not a summery day, I titled this picture of straw hats for sale, 'women waiting for summer to arrive.'"

Photography Contest Winner:
Takio Fukushima

● *Above*

A *danchi*, or modern apart-
ment-house development, in
a valley between Tokyo and
Mount Fuji.

Photographer:

Rick Smolan

**Picture Story
by Galen Rowell**

● *Right*

The road to Tateyama opens just before Golden Week in late April, when snow begins to melt and a series of three holidays—the Emperor's birth day, Constitution Day and Children's Day—bring many vacationers to the area.

● *Previous page*

Two hundred students from Jiyu Gakuen, a Tokyo private college, on their annual three-day mountain outing.

● *Above*

Even in June there is plenty of snow in Tateyama.

● *Right*

Jiyu Gakuen students pose at the summit of a 3,015-meter (9,892-foot) peak in the Tateyama mountain range in central Honshu.

● *Left*

Start of *tsuyu*, the rainy season, Japan's late-spring month of chill and gloom. The *tsuyu* starts in the south and works its way toward northern Honshu. By June 7, it had already reached the Tokiwa Bridge over the Abu River in Hagi City.

Photographer:

James Nachtwey

● *Above*

Tokoji Temple in Hagi City, said to have the biggest collection of stone lanterns in the world. Photographer Nachtwey made his shot through a plastic umbrella.

Photographer:

James Nachtwey

YOMIURI

Kanazawa, Ishikawa Prefecture   Michael Melfor

Tokyo   Gary Chapman

Kamakura, Kanagawa Prefecture   Jay Maisel

Tokyo   Mark S. Wexle

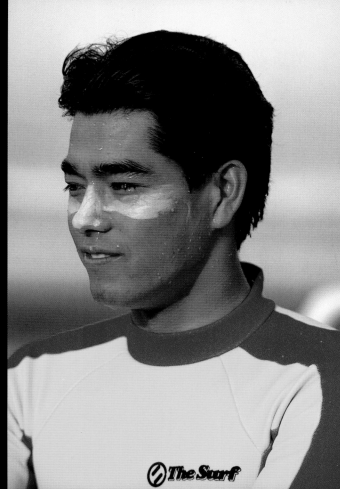

Torami Beach, Chiba Prefecture   Aaron Chang

● *Above, top*

An Ohazama kindergarten.

Photographer:
Ian Lloyd

● *Above*

Volunteer firefighters in
Ohazama.

Photographer:
Ian Lloyd

● *Right*

Rear Admiral Makoto Suzuki,
superintendent of the
Maritime Self Defense Force
training school at Etajima,
near Hiroshima, leads officer
cadets in saluting the flag. Pro-
spective officers for all three
Japanese services graduate
from the Defense Academy at

Yokosuka, near Tokyo, and
then proceed to specialized
officer-candidate schools. Navy
cadets have studied at Etajima
since 1888.

Photographer:
P. F. Bentley

Picture Story
by Nicole Bengevino

Unlike photographer Nicole Bengevino, few visitors to Japan will ever see members of the Japanese Self Defense Forces, and fewer still will recognize them as military personnel. Officers wear civilian clothes on the street, military parades are all but invisible and no Japanese tank or artillery piece has been seen in a big city for 40 years.

Why the shyness? To begin with, some Japanese still consider the armed forces to be illegal under the terms of Japan's American-drafted Constitution which states that "the Japanese people forever renounce war as a sovereign right of the nation" and that "land, sea and air forces, as well as other war potential, will never be maintained."

Today, Japan does indeed maintain armed forces which are small, well-equipped and, above all, unagressive. To make the argument clearer, they are called "self defense forces," never army, navy or air force.

Some Japanese politicians would like to rewrite the Constitution and build a military presence more commensurate with Japan's economic status. However, a strong section of public opinion remembers and resents the conduct of the former Japanese Imperial Army. This group prefers today's low-profile force—as do Japan's neighbors in Asia. Making war brought Japan to the edge of unimaginable disaster in 1945, while making cars, ships and televisions has brought respect abroad and unprecedented prosperity at home.

The post-war military have worked hard to earn public support by rushing help to communities struck by floods, typhoons and earthquakes, and by such public-spirited projects as cleaning up garbage left on Mount Fuji. As a further way of humanizing their image, all three Japanese armed services have been recruiting women since 1974, something unthinkable in the old Imperial Army.

The atmosphere of today's Japanese services is very different from the old style. Officers use polite language to enlisted men and women, and there is none of the face slapping and brutal field punishment that characterized the Imperial forces.

● *Below and right*

Japan's servicewomen are paid the same wages as their male colleagues, and one has already reached the rank of lieutenant colonel.

The Self Defense Forces do not intend to use women in combat, but recruits are ex- pected to know basic prin- ciples. Women's training also covers many non-combat topics.

Photographer:
Nicole Bengevino

Basic training is over and recruits hear their assignments. They will join different units all over Japan. Some in tears, they salute the national flag and shout, "Now the tests are over.... Our placements are decided.... We're going to do a good job in the future."
Photographer:
Nicole Bengevino

June 7, 1985, was the last day of basic infantry training for 191 young women at the Ground Self Defense Force base at Asaka, near Tokyo. Women can enlist at age 18, with a two-year initial commitment. All have patriotic motives, but many young women also want job security, a driving license (which can cost a Japanese civilian ¥ 300,000 or US$1,200 in driving-school fees), office skills and a military husband. The services run their own matrimonial agencies, and a girl would have to be unlucky indeed not to find a suitable husband in the ranks. As most women recruits expect to marry, they are taught flower arranging, the tea ceremony and other accomplishments thought useful for a future bride.

Left

Tokyo fireman in full regalia oes door to door checking for aky pipes after a neighborood gas explosion.

hotographer:
erd Ludwig

地震 火を消せ!!

ゆさゆさ

● *Above*

On September 1, 1923, the worst earthquake of this century left Tokyo and Yokohama in ruins. Much of the damage was caused by fires resulting from gas leaks. Since then, Japanese fire departments have been conducting drills to educate the public about emergency procedures.

On June 7th, Shibamata schoolchildren and their mothers participated in an earthquake drill organized by the Kanamachi fire department. A cut-away kitchen mounted on the back of a flatbed truck served as the stage. While two mothers and their children sat in the kitchen, a simulated earthquake caused the room to shake and shudder. The children and their mothers practiced turning off the gas stove, water heater and electric heater, and quickly finding shelter under the kitchen table. The children had difficulty taking the whole affair seriously, but as the children stepped down from the truck, the firemen solemnly handed each child a card (*left*) certifying that he had passed the drill.

Photographer:
Rick Smolan

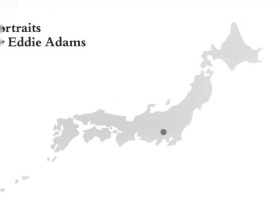

● *Left and below*

The Japanese word for love is *ai*, and so Aikawa-cho translates as "Love River Town." Actually, Aikawa (pop. 6,120) is more of a village, tucked away in the Tanzawa mountains. The Jomon people, forerunners of the Japanese, once built their campfires here. In 1569, a great battle was fought nearby between two fierce clans, the Takeda and the Hojo. When World War II ended, General MacArthur landed at nearby Atsugi airfield.

Apart from these historic events, nothing much has happened in Aikawa in the past few thousand years. The mon-soon rains of early summer fall on forested mountains where the Shoguns used to hunt. Deer and monkeys still venture out from the forest to rob the villagers' gardens. People grow mulberry trees, cultivate radishes, brew *sake*, cut lumber, are born, marry, move away, and sometimes come home to die. So Aikawa is a *furusato*, the ancestral village almost all Japanese have somewhere in their backgrounds and hold high in their affections.

Pulitzer Prize winner Eddie Adams has spent a great deal of his life photographing wars and famines. On June 7, 1985, he set up a studio in the Komaya Inn, on the banks of the Love River. Then he invited residents to have their pictures taken. Myoshin Nakamura came. At 82 she is Aikawa's leading artist. She moved to Aikawa from Tokyo when her house was demolished to make way for the 1964 Olympics. She liked the life and never moved back. She writes poetry, composes songs and teaches calligraphy to the local children. Nakamura wrote a song about Adams' visit, the biggest news in Aikawa for years. She also painted the character for "love" on Adams' backdrop.

Tadoka Hori, *village beauty, age 6*

Kenichiro Tsuchiya, *poultry supplier*

Sada Suzuki, *sporty grandma*

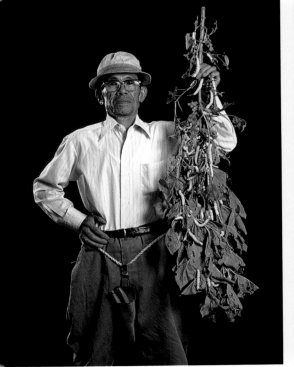

Keiji Yamaguchi, *silk farmer*

Shizue Ogawa, *midwife*

Akio Osawa, *fishmonger*

Diego Goldberg

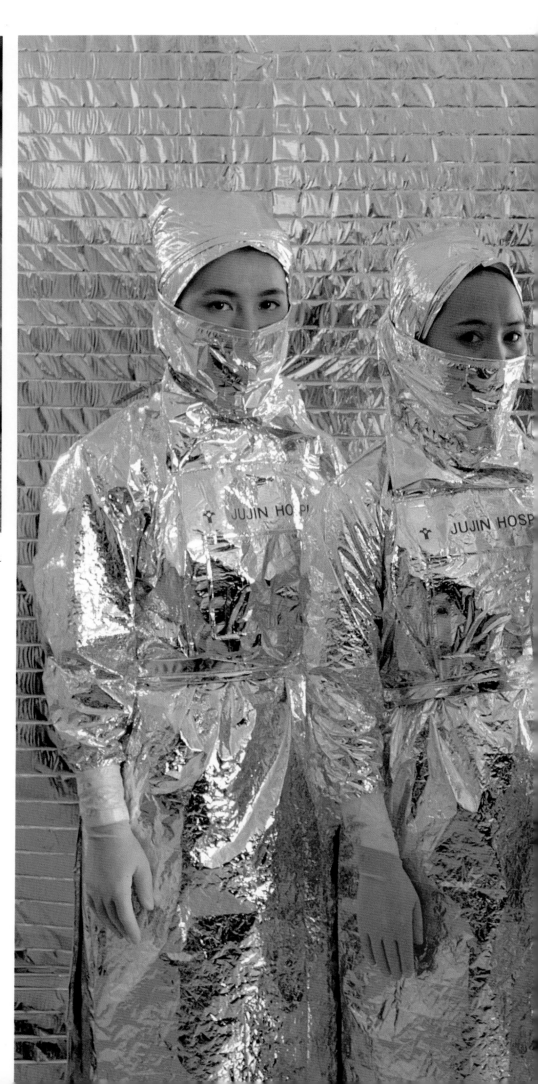

● *Previous page*

No matter the time of day or night, Japanese vending machines are ready to serve you with nearly anything you desire. Whether it's hot *sake*, iced coffee, hot noodles, a quart of whiskey, or a copy of the latest magazine, the vending machines are a permanent fixture of the Japanese landscape. Many of them even have a computer chip that says "Thank you" as your selection pops out. For ¥ 100 (US$.40) you can get a Kirin Mets, Coke or Pepsi. In other vending machines, a beer costs from ¥ 180 (US$.70) for a can to ¥ 1,500 (US$6) for a plastic two-litre keg. These machines were photographed in Hokkaido.

Photographer:

Diego Goldberg

● *Above and right*

The Jujin Hospital in Tokyo is Japan's best-known center for cosmetic surgery, specializing in face lifts, new noses and augmented bosoms. Jujin's head surgeon, Dr. Umezawa, shows the mold of a patient's new face.

Much has been made in the foreign press about operations that westernize Japanese eyes. The hospital occasionally accommodates patients, mostly bar hostesses and would-be fashion models, who want their eyelids and noses altered to look more Western. But the overwhelming number of Japanese are quite content the way they are.

Photographer:

Mark S. Wexler

● *Above, top*

The famous *torii* gate at Miyajima, near Hiroshima. The original shrine was built in 593. The present gate was erected in 1875.

Photographer:

Eikoh Hosoe

● *Above*

Fukuura, Aomori Prefecture.

Photographer:

Lynn Johnson

● *Right*

A *kendo* instructor in traditional gear at the Maritime Self Defense Force training school in Etajima.

Photographer:

P.F. Bentley

● *Left*

Giant straw *waraji* sandals on the wall of the Kotokuin Temple in Kamakura symbolize the wandering life of the Buddhist teacher.

Photographer:

Jay Maisel

● *Above*

Hands of the *Daibutsu*, the 122-ton statue of the Buddha in Kamakura. According to tradition, the Buddha's hands were in this position when He achieved enlightenment.

Photographer:

Jay Maisel

● *Following page*

Students of Ajigasawa Second Junior High School posed together for a yearbook photo. When it came time to break ranks, the girls were dismissed first.

Photographer:

Lynn Johnson

Picture Story
by Rudi Meisel

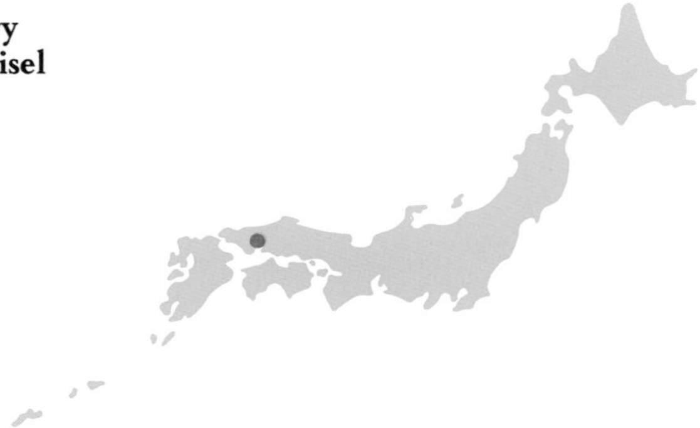

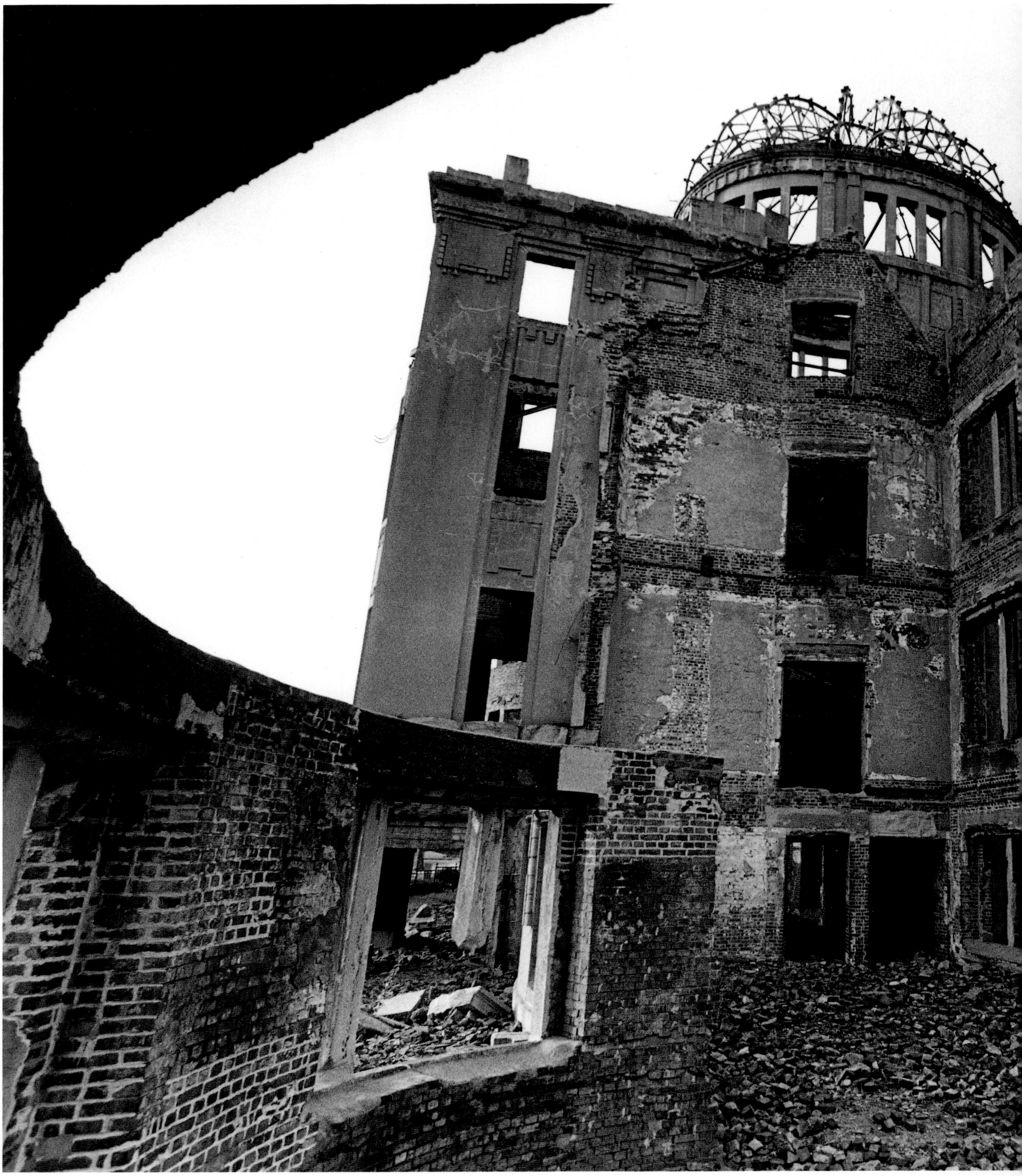

● *Left*

On August 6, 1945, the city
of Hiroshima was all but
wiped out in the world's first
atomic attack. On June 7,
forty years later, West German
photographer Rudi Meisel
wandered around the city
which has been completely
rebuilt.

"It was a disturbing ex-
perience," he reported. "We
Germans have a lot of trouble
with the memories of 40 years
back, too." Meisel was born
in Hamburg, West Germany,
another city destroyed from
the air.

"I wanted to photograph
Hiroshima as just another city,
but what I found instead was a
city that had made a cottage
industry out of disaster. The
first thing I saw was a group
of children drawing the ruined
Industry Promotion Hall, now
called the Atom Bomb Dome.
It was left standing as a mem-
orial, and every day groups of
students are herded by to take
a look. Then a local television
crew introduced me to some
survivors, and I was reluctant
to look into their faces. I asked
if I could photograph their
wounded hands, and they said,
'Of course, that's why we're
here,' as if they were professional victims. I photographed
the mayor, Mr. Araki, who
was also a survivor of the
blast.

"Later, I found a big room
at the University of Hiroshima
where they have jars filled
with the skin and organs of
people who were killed by the
bomb. Originally, they were
kept for research, and now no
one knows what to do with
them. I said, 'Why keep these
things here? Why not send
them to Washington where
they might do some good?'"

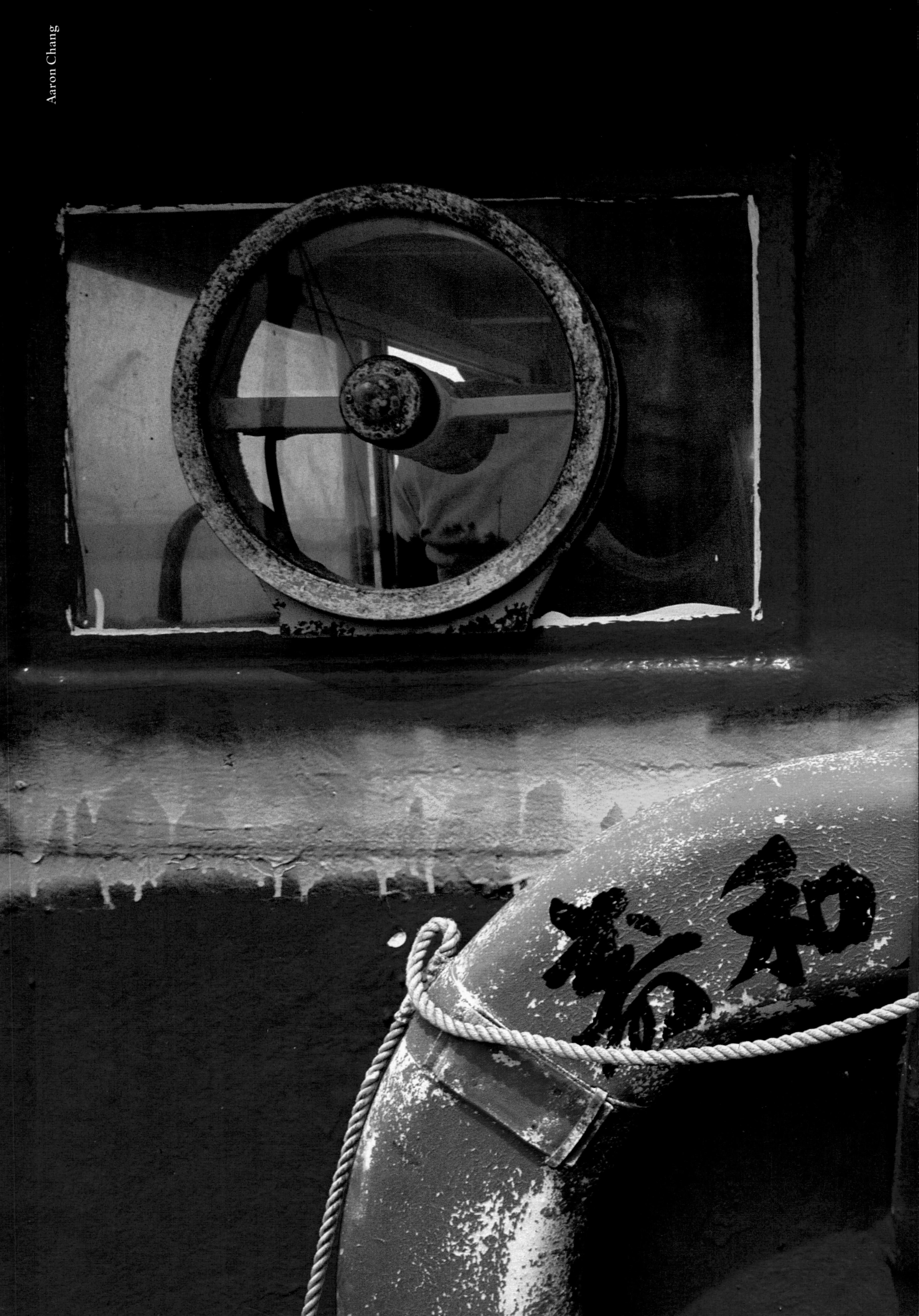

Aaron Chang

● *Previous page*

Chiba Prefecture.

Photographer:
Aaron Chang

● *Left and below*

The waters off Japan's Kerama Islands are high in oxygen, slightly cold and especially rich in coral. David Doubilet, considered to be one of the world's finest underwater photographers, and who's dived in six of its seven seas, says, "This underwater life is some of the most spectacular I've ever seen."

Photographer:
David Doubilet

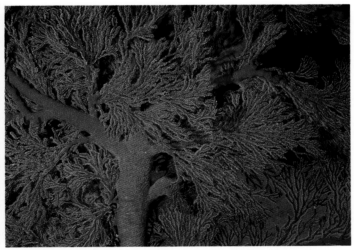

Nikko, Tochigi Prefecture   Kazuyoshi Nomachi

Kushiro, Hokkaido   Kent Kobersteen

Tatebayashi, Gunma Prefecture   Yuji Tsukada Yubari, Hokkaido

Ueno Park, Tokyo — John Keating

Chiba City, Chiba Prefecture — Hiroyuki Matsumoto

Tottori Sand Dunes — Maddy Miller

Teshikega-cho, Hokkaido — Jack Corn

Kochi, Shikoku — Seigi Uemura

● *Left*

Yukio Kubo, 36, has delivered lunch orders to Akihabara offices and shops for 15 years. Here, he balances 50 boxes of *soba* (buckwheat noodles) weighing 30 kilograms (66 pounds).

Photographer:
Kaku Kurita

● *Above*

Workers prepare *bento*, popular Japanese boxed lunches, at Nippon Shokudo, one of the largest *bento* factories in a country that often eats lunch on the run. Simple *bento* are sold on railway platforms and in department stores. Very elaborate *bento* are served at weddings and funerals.

Photographer:
Mark S. Wexler

● *Left, top*

American fast foods are now served in most Japanese cities. The sign says, "*Makudonarudo* is the world language."

Photographer:
Bill Pierce

● *Below*

Lia Mays, daughter of a Japanese mother and an American serviceman father, serves chicken in Okinawa. The Colonel Sanders Kentucky Fried Chicken operation in Japan is half-owned by the huge Mitsubishi concern.

Photographer:
Eli Reed

● *Above*

Japanese *purasuchikku foodo*. Lifelike plastic food models are shown in the windows of most Japanese restaurants, enabling Japanese to decide what they want to eat and foreigners to place their orders by pointing. Earlier models, made of wax, had an unappetizing tendency to melt in the hot sun. Originally the models were made to resemble the food, but these days the food has to live up to the promise of the models.

Photographer:
Joy Wolf

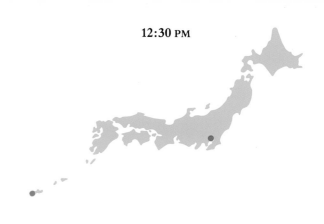

● *Previous page, left and below*

In spring 1985, Japanese industry and government staged Expo '85 at Tsukuba Science City near Tokyo. While somewhat disappointing as a showcase of Japanese technology, Tsukuba proved popular with tourists and children. A young Korean photographer, Koo Bohn-Chang, brought his camera and a fresh eye to what must have been Japan's most photographed subject of 1985.

Picture Story
by Koo Bohn-Chang

In June 1972, *Life* magazine published one of the most famous articles in the history of photojournalism, W. Eugene Smith's picture essay on the small fishing village of Minamata.

Minamata Disease now stands for a whole family of maladies. All were caused by pollution of air, water and soil, a byproduct of Japan's explosive, often reckless industrial growth in the 1950s and 1960s. Early in this period, the Chisso Corporation introduced a new process for synthesizing acetaldehyde (an ingredient of vinyl) at its plant at Minamata on Kyushu. The effluent, which contained mercury, was dumped without treatment into Minamata Bay.

In 1953, fishermen and their families began to show signs of a previously unknown disease. Symptoms included loss of hearing and sight, paralysis and mental disorders in adults and, even more tragically, mental handicaps and severe birth defects in children. In 1971, the mercury level near the company's drainage outlet was found to be 2,000 times the safe limit.

By 1981, the number of confirmed cases had risen to 1,293, with 305 dead, and Chisso, after a bitter court case, had paid out ¥51.6 billion (US$200 million) in compensation. By June 7, 1985, more than 15,000 people had filed claims.

Some good did come out of Minamata. Fishing in the bay was banned in 1973, and no new cases of the disease have been recorded since. In that year, Japan also began a massive nation-wide campaign against pollution. Incidence of pollution diseases have been drastically reduced, the air and water of Japanese cities have been spectacularly improved, fish have returned to the rivers and Japan is now the world's major exporter of pollution-control equipment. But the price of Japan's economic miracle in twisted bodies and wrecked lives has been high, and many innocent victims, like these, are still paying it.

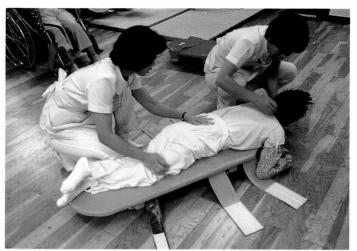

● *Left and below*

Eugene Smith was not the first to photograph Minamata. Japanese photographer Shisei Kuwabara went there in 1960 and later published two picture books. On June 7, 1985, Kuwabara revisited Minamata to record the progress being made by victims of the disease at the Meisuien rehabilitation facility.

● *Left*

Osaka motorcycle police preparing for a group portrait. Like the Los Angeles police, they ride Japanese motorcycles.

Photographer:

Roger Ressmeyer

● *Above, top and bottom*

Riot police at the trial of gangsters belonging to the notorious *Yamaguchi-gumi* gang at an Osaka courthouse. Japan has at least 120,000 full-time professional gangsters belonging to 2,500 separate gangs. *Yamaguchi-gumi*, which originated in Kobe, is the biggest. Japanese organized crime tends to be highly organized. The location of *Yamaguchi-gumi* headquarters is public knowledge and even listed in the telephone directory.

Back at the office hoodlums keep watch inside and out. Japanese gangsters are called *yakuza*, which roughly translates as "worthless." They operate protection rackets, deal in drugs, extortion and "labor relations" and occasionally resort to murder —mostly of each other.

Photographer:

Abbas

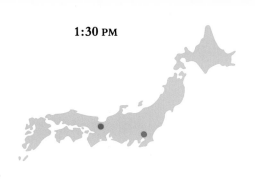

● *Left*
Tattoo artist Horihiro Akasaka
of Kawaguchi City, Saitama
Prefecture, works on a living
canvas. Tatooing in Japan is
most popular among *yakuza*
(members of Japanese organized crime groups), but it is an
ancient Japanese folk art, and
some Japanese with no *yakuza*
connections sport elaborate
decorations.
Photographer:
Lucy Birmingham

● *Above*
Dr. Toshiyasu Shimizu makes
a house call in Yonaguni
Village, Okinawa Prefecture.
Photographer:
Greg Davis

● *Following page*
Mourners at a Kyoto funeral.
Photographer:
Jodi Cobb

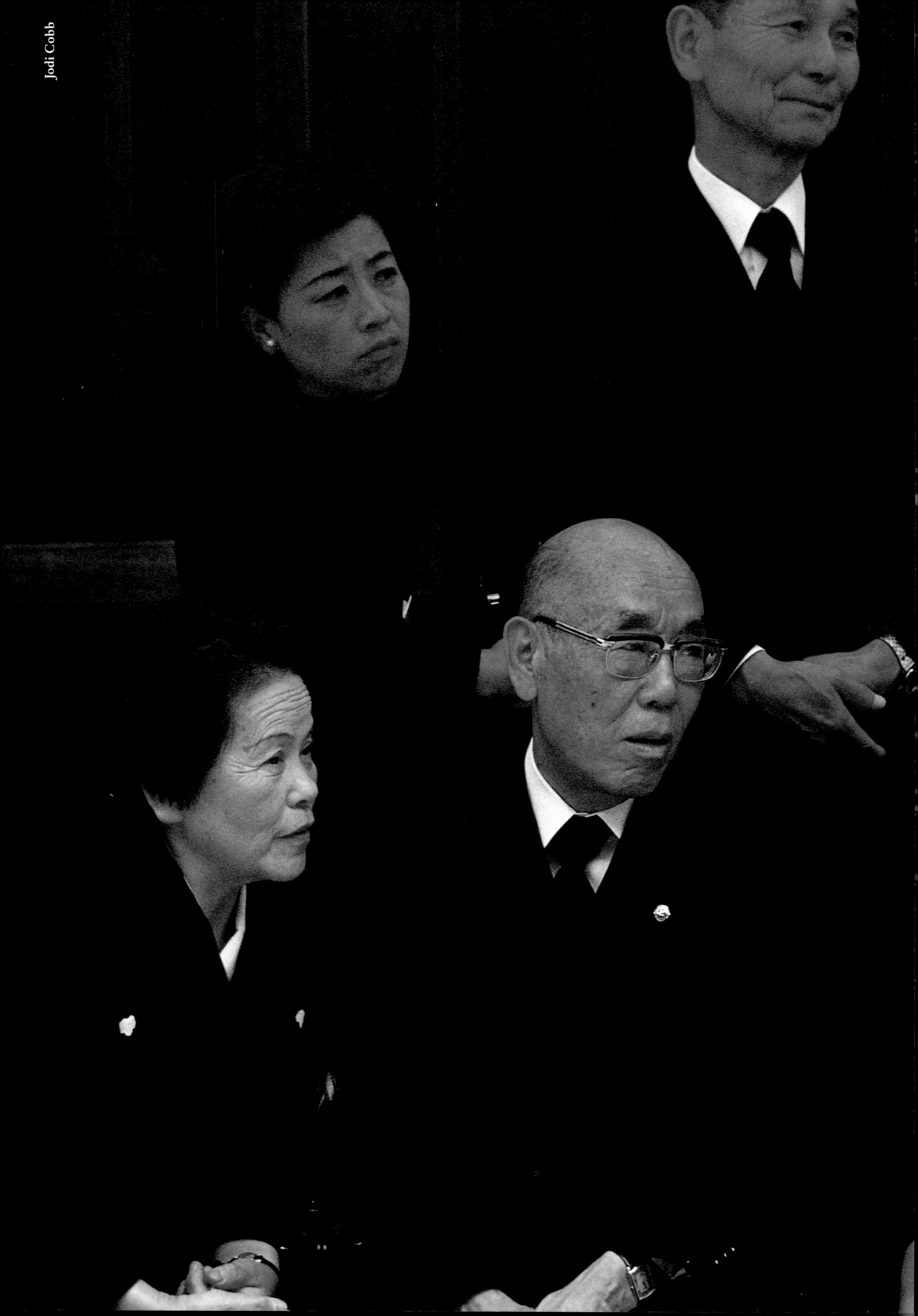

Jodi Cobb

Fukuura, Aomori Prefecture

Lynn Johnson

Chiba City

Hiroyuki Matsumoto

Kushiro, Hokkaido

Jennifer Erwitt

Kamakura, Kanagawa Prefecture

Jay Maisel

aha, Okinawa

Takeji Iwamiya

MEN

Chiba Prefecture

Aaron Chan

S umo, the most authentically Japanese sport, began as a religious exercise. At the dawn of Japanese history, young men wrestled in the courtyards of *Shinto* shrines to amuse the gods. Japan's Emperor Hirohito, once regarded as a god himself, is a lifelong *sumo* fan and regularly attends the *basho* or tournaments. Like most Japanese, he also follows *sumo* in the comfort of his home.

Although encrusted with centuries-old ceremony, *sumo* is just right for television. After 4 minutes of ritual stamping, squatting, puffing and throwing of salt (for purity), the actual wrestling usually lasts 20 seconds. If there is no decision after a few minutes, the wrestlers stop for a rest. Television videotape can slow down or stop the furious action, compare one style with another and show the subtle differences between the 48 recognized throws and holds.

The brevity of the action does not mean, however, that Japan's 700-odd professional *sumotori* are a crowd of overfed, out-of-shape sissies. Far from it. *Sumo* is a tough sport, and careers are generally short

Below

Sumotori train by lunging at a *teppo*—a bare wooden pole which serves as the *sumotori's* punching bag—until their hands and forearms are as hard as clubs. They also work out with weights (a recent development) and spend hours doing squats and other exercises to develop steely muscles under their blubber.

● *Right*

The 4.55-meter (14.9-foot) *sumo* ring is made of packed clay, which is as hard as concrete. A wrestler wins by forcing his opponent out of the ring or causing him to touch the ground with any part of his body other than the soles of his bare feet.

and painful. Every Japanese schoolboy with a double chin dreams of a *sumo* career. But for most of them, the reality would be (apart from all the eating and drinking) a monkish young manhood full of sprains, bruises and broken bones, compulsory retirement before the age of 30, and dreary years of dieting to get back into shape for a regular job. Only a fortunate few go on to become champions (*ozeki*) or grand champion (*yokozuna*), multimillionaires and national heroes.

June 7, 1985, fell between major tournaments —there are only six in Japan each year—but training went on as usual. Mark S. Wexler visited three stables in Tokyo to photograph young hopefuls taking their first massive steps on the road to fame, fat and fortune.

● *Above*

After working out on the *teppo*, a young *sumotori* tests his forearm on a softer target. *Sumotori* are not permitted to punch or kick, but they achieve much the same result with *tsuppari*, slapping their opponents about the head and shoulders.

Great bulk, great strength and a low center of gravity are all assets, and *sumotori* achieve their size by eating bowl after bowl of "wrestler's stew" (*chanko-nabe*) with mounds of boiled rice washed down with endless bottles of beer and *sake*.

● *Right*

Entry into the profession is tough and humiliating. Apprentices have to sweep out the training stable, wait on tables and tend to the elaborate hairstyles of the established wrestlers, as well as suffer a full day's training. Beginners are wretchedly paid and cannot think of marrying until they have fought their way up the ranks. (The baby is a visitor.)

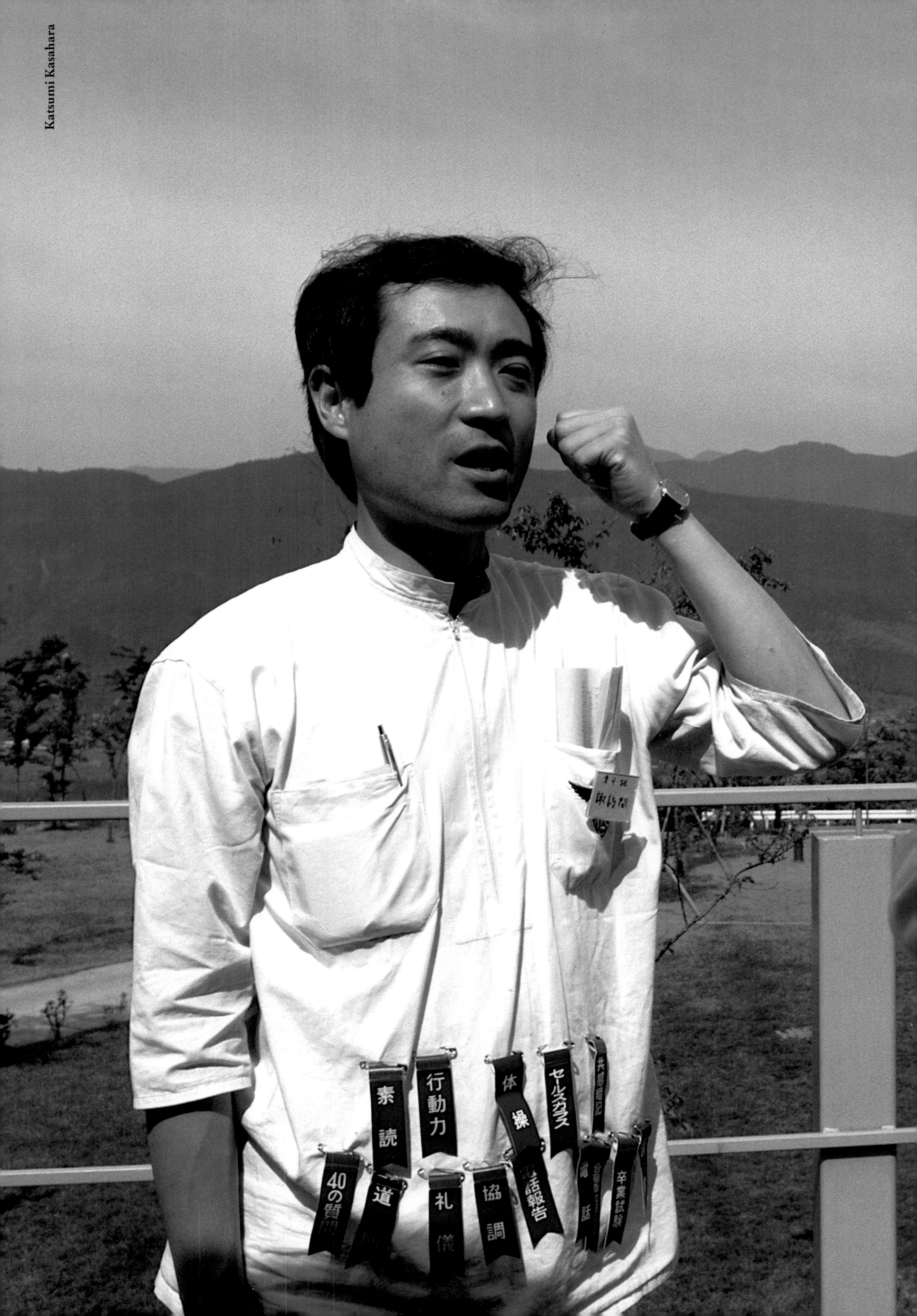

Katsumi Kasahara

Picture Story
by Katsumi Kasahara

● *Previous page*

At the famous Management Training School near Mount Fuji students practice making the perfect telephone call. The ribbons are for the subjects the student still has to pass. Some students burst into tears and hug their instructors' feet when they graduate.

● *Left and above*

The basic concept behind the Management Training School is to break down traditional Japanese reserve and politeness and turn the graduates into forceful, hard-driving salesmen and managers. The atmosphere is midway between Marine boot camp and a Dale Carnegie uplift course. The 13-day session covers such topics as assertiveness, salesmanship, team spirit, business etiquette and the English language (which largely consists of learning to sing "I Did It My Way"). Some physical exercises are included, in particular, one to strengthen the stomach muscles for more forceful selling and order-giving. Students, many senior executives sent by their companies, are required to scrub the floor and clean up the school with the same energy. It is, in fact, spotless.

• *Above and right*

The famous hot volcanic-sand baths at Surigahama on the southern tip of Kyushu island. Attendants shovel sand, which is heavy and stiflingly hot (29.4°C/85°F), over visitors. The treatment is said to be slimming and good for rheumatism, arthritis and whatever else ails you. Twenty minutes is about as long as even the toughest invalid can stand.

Photographer:
Mike Yamashita

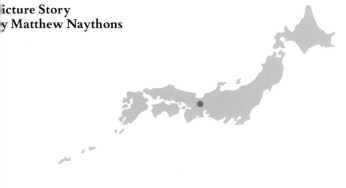

Buddhism is the only foreign religion that has ever put down deep roots in Japan. Less than 1 percent of Japanese, for instance, practice Christianity. In the days of the Shoguns—until 1868—Buddhist observance was compulsory, and today nearly 90 percent of all Japanese still belong to one or more of the 13 major Buddhist sects. (Most Japanese combine their Buddhism with *Shinto*, Japan's indigenous religion.)

Although historically important, the majority of Japanese have contact with Buddhist institutions only at funerals and festivals, or when they visit departed relatives at cemeteries. But Buddhism is still kept very much alive in Japan by professionals, as it has been for more than 1,400 years since the faith was introduced from India and China via Korea. On June 7, 1985, Japan had 252,200 full-time Buddhist priests, monks and nuns. Photographer Matthew Naythons visited the monastery of one of the oldest and strictest sects, *Tendai*, on sacred Mount Hiei, near Kyoto.

● *Left, above top and above*

The followers of *Tendai* seek nirvana through meditation and prayer. The forms of meditation are strenuous and often involve arduous repetition of monotonous physical tasks. One of the toughest activities (and therefore most valuable, from a spiritual point of view) is the "thousand-day walk" in which the seeker after enlightenment tramps 38,400 kilometers (24,000 miles), the equivalent of a stroll around the world. He follows thousand-year-old trails which crisscross the slopes of Mount Hiei, near Kyoto, meditating on the futility of earthly desire. During his marathon walk, the pilgrim wears out a pair of rice-straw sandals every two days.

Another form of *Tendai* observance is the endless raking of the graveled surface of the monastery's stone garden.

A third is the *goma*, or fire ceremony, in which sticks inscribed with prayers are burnt before an image of the Buddha. This ritual has been traced back more than 2,000 years to Indo-Iranian fire worship.

● *Far left*

Fashion designer Yohji Yamamoto in his Aoyama studio in Tokyo. In June 1985, Yamamoto was designing wide, comfortable clothing for men and women.

Photographer:

Gerd Ludwig

● *Left*

Rumiko Sato is spending ov ¥ 7,000 (US$28) to get the latest Japanese hair fashion, a *sutoreto paama* or ''straight perm.'' By Western standard most Japanese hair is straight already, but to achieve the glossy doll-like look, fashion able young women go to salons like ''Beauty Yokota,' on the outskirts of Tokyo.

Photographer:

Andy Levin

Below

t Hanae Mori's atelier in
Omote-sando, the high-
ashion center of Tokyo,
models display contemporary
imono designed by Nobuo
Nakamura of Kyoto. The
rices of these elegant crea-
ons range from ¥200,000
(US$800) to more than
¥1,000,000 (US$4,000).
hotographer:
orin Boyd

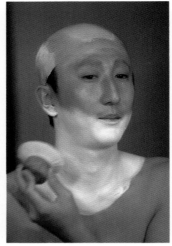
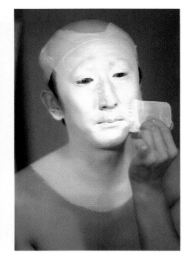

● *Above, top*
Nakamura Tokizo V makes up for a male role. *Kabuki* actors, the aristocracy of the Japanese stage, are awarded the names of distinguished predecessors.

● *Above*
Four young actors, who have not yet achieved professional names, dressed as low-class prostitutes for the play *Sukeroku*. The setting is Yoshiwara, the former brothel district of Tokyo (now a center for massage parlors). Their *obi* sashes are back-to-front, indicating their profession.

● *Right*
Nakamura Tokizo V dressing for a female role, that of the courtesan Shiratama in *Sukeroku*.

Developed during the centuries of isolation (1639–1854), *kabuki* is uniquely Japanese and one of the world's great theatrical traditions. It began modestly enough with singing, dancing and comic sketches performed on the dry bed of the Kamo River in Kyoto by a mostly female troupe led by a Shinto priestess. (Hence its name, which means "song dance skill.") Featuring erotic dancing and off-color jokes, the original "women's *kabuki*" was a roaring success, leading to fist-fights among the audience over the favors of the entertainers, who may have practiced prostitution on the side. To stop these disorders, Shogun Iemitsu Tokugawa banned female entertainers from *kabuki* performances. The young boys who took over all the women's roles were banned for similar reasons in 1652. Ironically, the puritanical military government of the Shogun gave *kabuki* its most enduring and popular feature, the *onnagata* or male actors who play female parts with a delicacy and refinement few women—even Japanese—can match.

Kabuki matured as the people's theater of Edo (now Tokyo), the Shogun's capital. Edo-ites wanted excitement and laughs, and the lofty (and, to many, boring) high art of the classical *noh* drama was reserved for the ruling class. *Kabuki* responded with melodramatic plots of betrayal and revenge, dazzling swordplay, the world's first revolving stage, fires (the "flowers of Edo"), typhoons and earthquakes, all before their very eyes.

When Japan finally opened up to the outside world, *kabuki* tried to move with the times and into modern dress. Many writers (including the Japanese novelist Yukio Mishima) attempted new plays. But to audiences, this *kabuki* was about as convincing as Shakespeare played in a three-piece suit. The old style quickly returned, and today's *kabuki* is the living Japan of the Shoguns, complete with cunning merchants, arrogant two-sworded samurai, suicidal lovers and stoic down-trodden farmers—fascinating to both Japanese and, via *kabuki*'s deep influence on Japanese films, the rest of the world.

● *Left*

The Far East meets the Old West at Tokyo Disneyland. Three generations of a Japanese family pose as American pioneers, complete with bonnets, a Winchester rifle replica and granny's sandals.

Photographer:

Dilip Mehta

● *Above*

Conventional amusement parks are experiencing stiff competition from Tokyo Disneyland, but a young patron of the Korakuen Amusement Center in central Tokyo can still laugh his head off.

Photographer:

Andy Levin

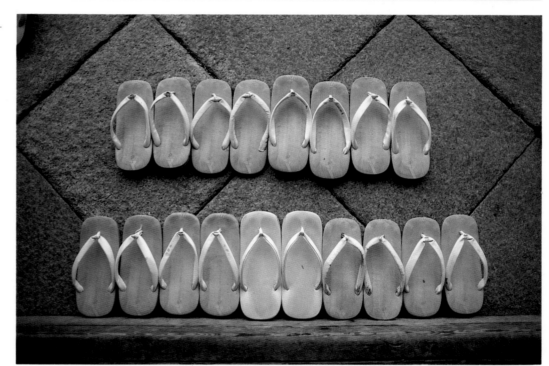

● *Left*

A visiting Cinderella finds her prince at Tokyo Disneyland.

Photographer:

Dilip Mehta

● *Right*

Japanese people take off their shoes when they enter the house, and visitors should too. The correct place is not outside the front door but in the *genkan*, or entrance hall. Some Japanese homes provide slippers to wear inside, and all have special slippers for the toilet. Toilet slippers in hotels often have "toilet" written in Japanese across the toes and should not be worn anywhere else.

These are the simple rules, but like most Japanese customs, things can get much more complicated. Japanese dentists wear slippers while drilling teeth, truck drivers often wear slippers on the road. Some Japanese office workers wear slippers (or sandals), some wear shoes. In early 1985, there was a controversy at the Japanese Ministry of Posts and Telecommunications when some employees wanted to wear slippers and some wanted to wear shoes. A typical Japanese compromise was reached when the director-general asked footwear manufacturers to design slippers that looked like shoes.

Photographers, top to bottom:

Matthew Naythons
José Azel
Mike Yamashita

● *Following page*

A head by two feet: soaking in a health-giving hot-spring pool near the Japan Sea in Fukuura. High iron content makes the water brown.

Photographer:

Lynn Johnson

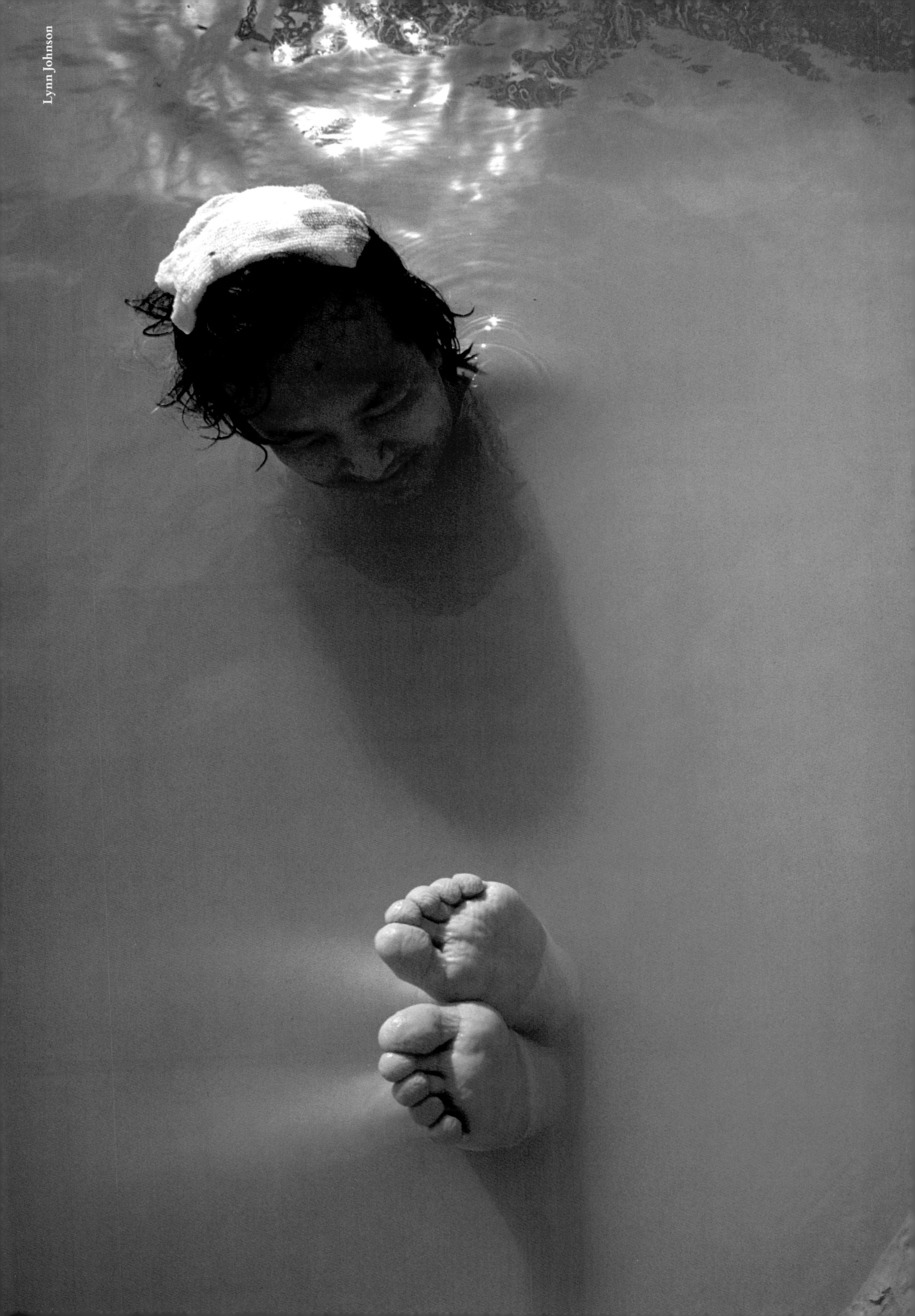

Lynn Johnson

eft

leo Kandachi cradles his son
r a long Friday at Tokyo
neyland. Japan was, and in
ny ways still is, an authori-
an society. As an old
anese saying put it, the four
igs for children to fear are
thquakes, lightning, fire
l father. But relationships
ween parents and children
changing in modern
an. In the past, fathers and

mothers were adddressed only
as *oto-san* and *oka-san* or
"respected father" and
"respected mother." By 1985,
terms such as "mama" and
"papa" had come into more
common use—English words
because there were no Japanese
words that expressed the same
intimacy.
Photographer:
Dilip Mehta

● *Left*
Urayasu.
Photographer:
Dilip Mehta

● *Above*
At the Fukuoka Zoo in
Kyushu, members of an all-
woman photography club take
pictures of a young model.
Photography Contest Winner:
Yoshiyuki Ueda

Kodak Japan K.K. and American Express International issued a challenge to amateur photographers: "Dust off your cameras on June 7 and match your photographic skills against 100 of the world's top photojournalists." A host of talented amateurs accepted the challenge and entered their best efforts in the Day in the Life of Japan photography contest. In some cases the amateur photographs were as good as or better than those taken by the professionals. Some of the winners are seen on this page. Others appear throughout the book.

Norihiko Miyata

Katsuyoshi Hasegawa

Sheunichi Munakata

Futami Sugawara

Children see the world with fresh eyes. On Friday, June 7, Kodak Japan K.K. supplied two hundred Japanese school children with Kodak Disc Cameras. In return for working on *A Day in the Life of Japan* the children were allowed to keep their cameras. On this page is a selection from the 9,600 photographs shot by this army of young photographers.

Yukiko Kuramochi, Age 10

Tomonori Nikaido, Age 10

Hiroki Itami, Age 7

Mayumi Kitagawa, Age 8

Yukiko Suzuki, Age 10

Ryugo Saejima, Age 8

● *Above*

Yoshihiro Oto, deputy mayor of Kanazawa (pop. 417,681), Ishikawa Prefecture, in the reception room of his office.
Photographer:
Michael Melford

● *Right and far right*

Prime Minister Yasuhiro Nakasone, an amateur painter, works briefly on a mountain landscape in the garden of his Tokyo official residence. Nakasone, who was born in 1918, once translated into Japanese a book about American techniques for winning elections. He has been a member of parliament since 1947 and head of government since December 1982. On June 7, 1985, he was able to spare 14 minutes to pose for photographer David Burnett (between a haircut and a meeting with a visiting member of the Chinese Council of State). Burnett had hoped for a leisurely private session but instead found what he called a "human wave" of Japanese photographers waiting to photograph *him* photographing the prime minister.
Photographer:
David Burnett

The chips are down: Hiroshi Mizuma with a circuit board at Seiko's Yatsu factory in Chiba Prefecture.

Photographer:
Arnaud de Wildenberg

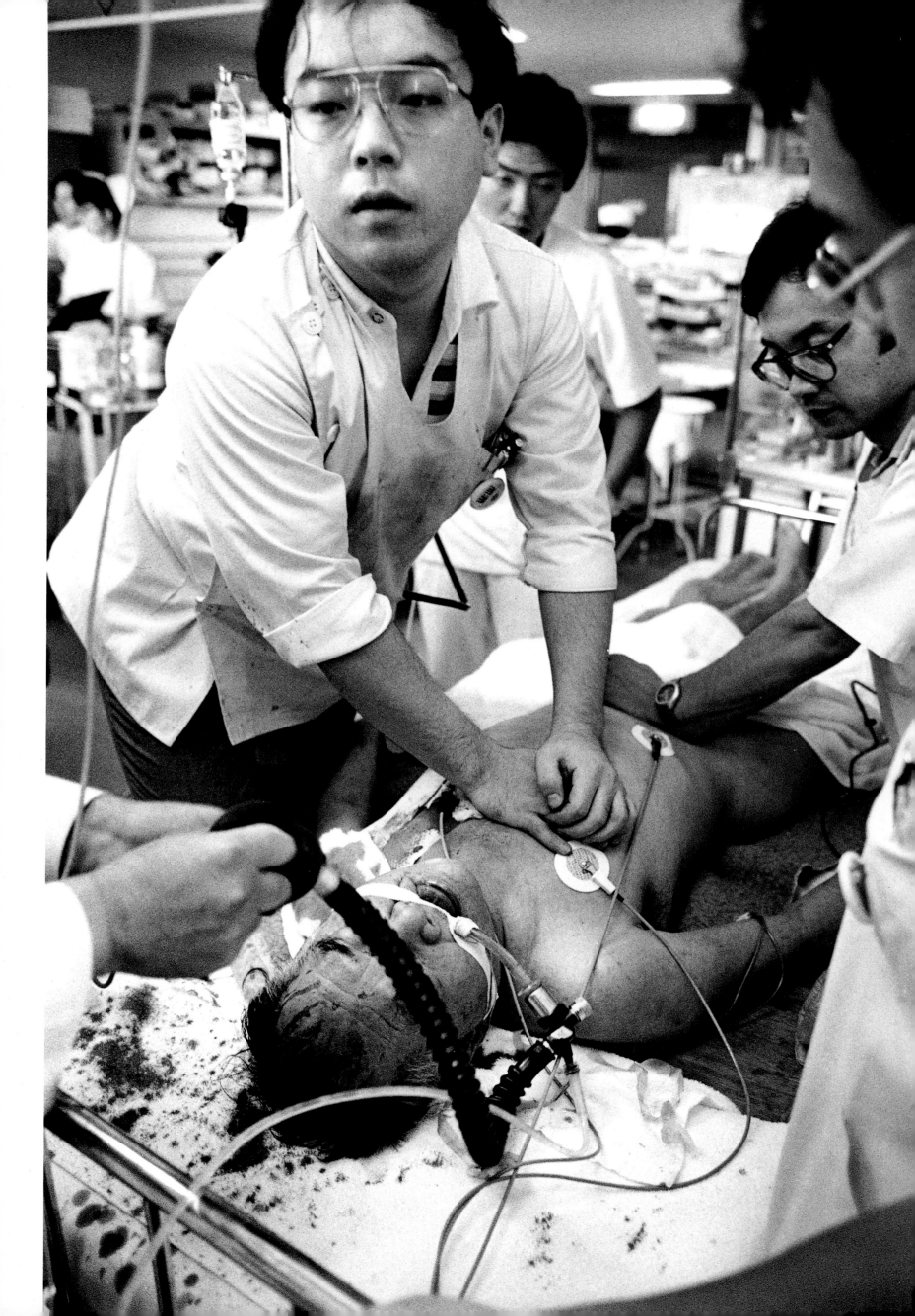

T wo days before he left for Japan, French photographer Jean-Pierre Laffont broke his leg while shooting publicity stills on a movie set Northern Africa. His original *Day in the Life of Japan* signment had been to spend the 7th of June in the byrinth of Tokyo's subway system. Instead, he spent e day taking photographs from a wheelchair in the aiseikai Byoin, a 736-bed general hospital in Shizuoka ity, southwest of Tokyo.

"My goal was to see if I could capture the ntire spectrum of hospital life from birth to death uring one 24-hour period. I come from a family of octors, so the sights and smells and sounds of a ospital aren't new or frightening to me. When I was ven I helped my father deliver a baby, so I grew up ery aware of the fragility of life and death.

"I have very strong memories from June 7th. was in the hall photographing some patients and the octors called me into the emergency room and said One of our patients is going into cardiac arrest!' There ere six doctors giving the man heart massage— ounting: one, two, three, four—taking turns for more an two hours. They tried so hard to keep this man ive, but despite their efforts he died.

"Being in a wheelchair was incredibly ustrating. I kept seeing things to photograph and ished I had the full use of my legs. But looking back I hink it actually helped me. Many of the people hought I was also a patient there. I was photographing group of handicapped children, and the moment the octors were out of sight the kids started racing up and own the corridor. I joined them even though they ere much faster than me.

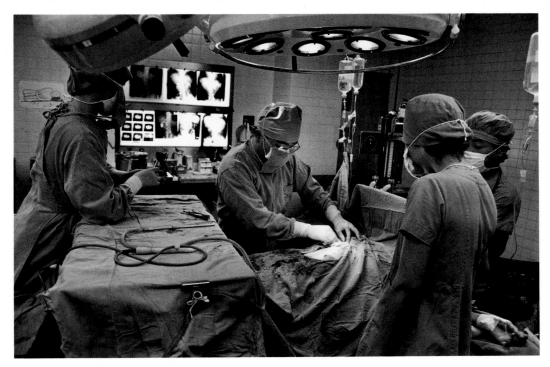

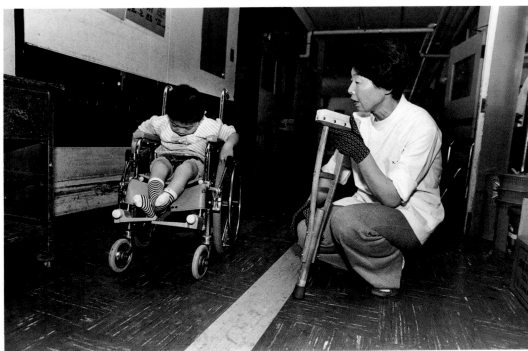

● *Above, top*

Entrance to the Saiseikai Byoin. Like most Japanese hospitals, it is privately owned. Nearly all Japanese are covered by health insurance (national or private) which pays most medical bills.

● *Above, middle*

An operation in progress. Japan has 122 physicians for every 100,000 persons, compared with 168 per 100,000 in the United States. Many physicians run one-doctor hospitals.

● *Above*

Three-year-old Kentaro Nanba recovering from a foot fractured in a traffic accident. Japanese children are often injured by cars while playing in narrow streets with no sidewalks. Japan is the only country in the world in which more people are killed *by* cars than *in* them.

153

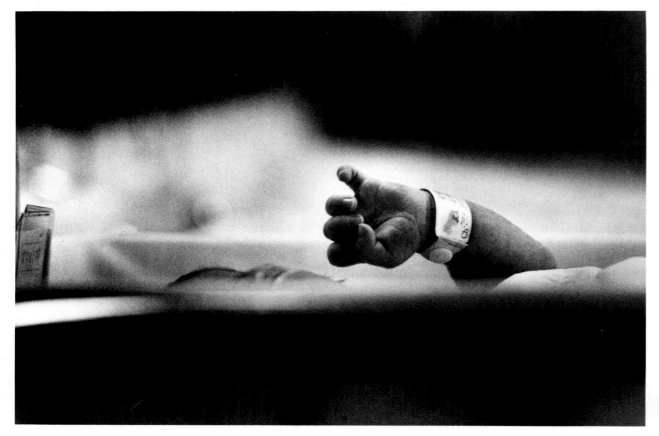

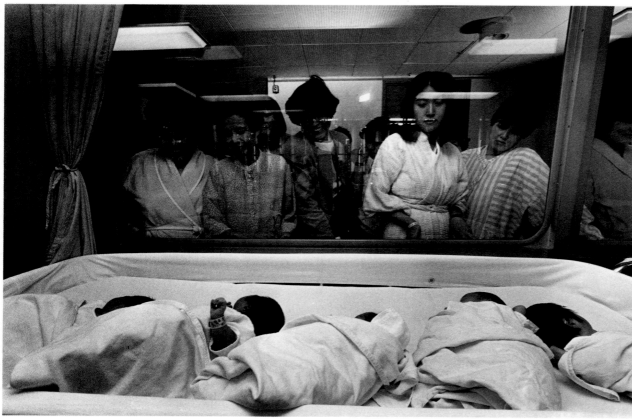

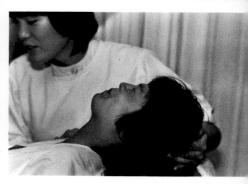

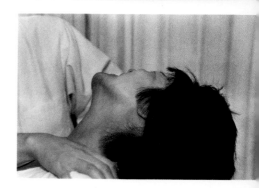

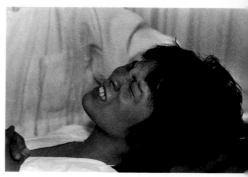

● *Above, top and bottom*

New arrivals at Tokyo Eisei Hospital. Childbirth is not classified as an illness by the Japanese national health system, and parents have to pay. Fees for an uncomplicated birth in a hospital range from ¥150,000 (US$600) in the country to ¥400,000 (US$1,600) at a fashionable Tokyo hospital. Japan has the lowest infant mortality rate in the world.

Photographer:
Masaaki Miyazawa

● *Right*

It's a *boya*! Labor and birth at Saiseikai Hospital in Shizuoka.

Photographer Jean-Pierre Laffont recalls, "My most memorable moment on June 7th was while I was photographing a childbirth. I was surprised that the moment the baby was born, he was given to his mother to hold against her skin, against her breast— so he could recognize the beating of his mother's heart. I've never seen that in Europe or the United States. And they stayed together like that, and the mother cried. It really touched me."

Photographer:
Jean-Pierre Laffont

154

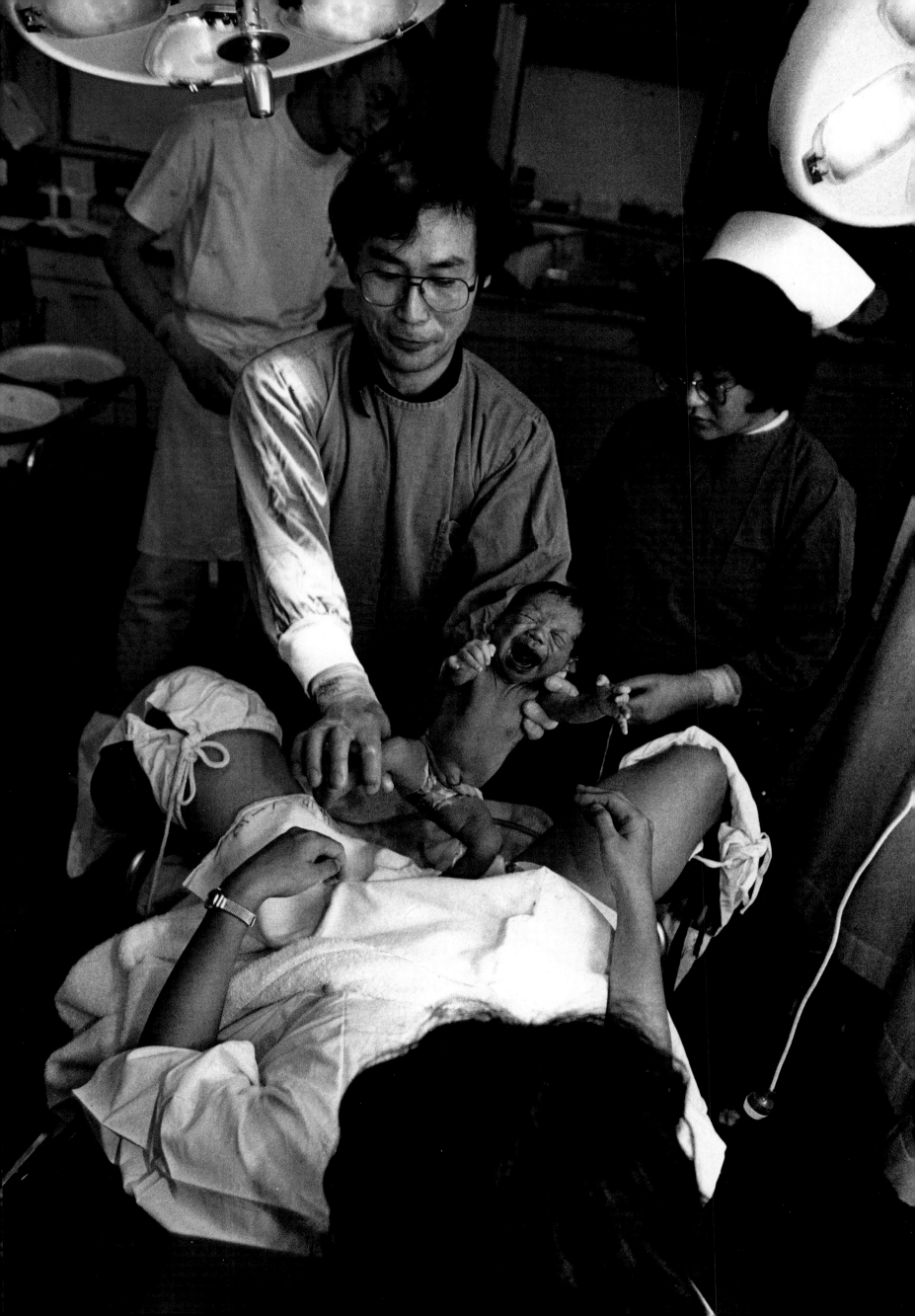

● *Above*

Although based on uniforms
worn by Prussian students in
the 1870s, Japanese high-
school clothing has no military
connotations. Some students
dislike them, but mothers find
them practical.

Photographer:
Lynn Johnson

● *Right*

Another uniform: Japanese
punks on the Doton-bori
Bridge in Osaka hand out
fliers for a new-wave club.
There are few natural blondes
in Japan.

Photographer:
Roger Ressmeyer

"I took this picture in Harajuku, Tokyo, a little after
4:00 in the afternoon on
June 7th. It was a hot day and
I happened to see a person taking a nap in an air-conditioned
coffee shop. I felt envious."
Photography Contest Winner:
Makoto Yamazaki

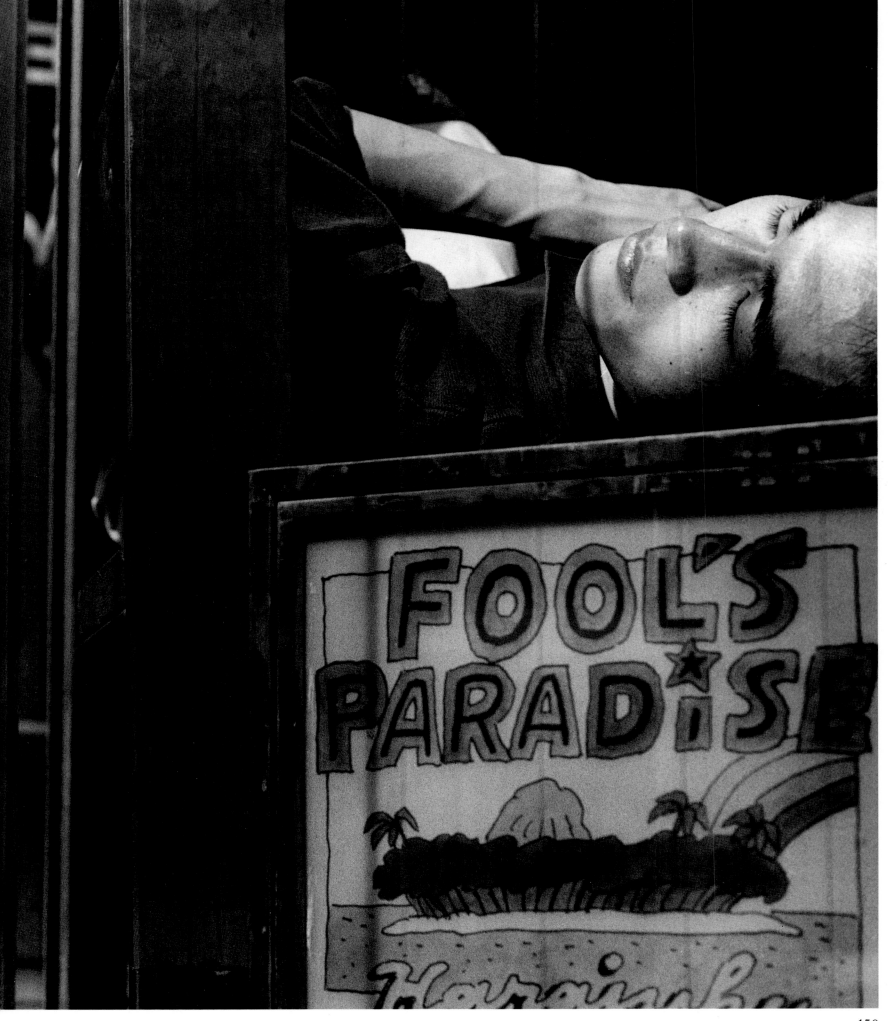

● *Left, top*

Mamoru Shimizu takes water to his teammates at a rugby game in Tokyo.

Photographer:

Gary Chapman

● *Left, below*

Biology class provokes fertile discussion among these Hokuyo High School students in Kushiro, Hokkaido.

Photographer:

Jennifer Erwitt

● *Below*

A stylish pass at an Osaka rugby game. Rugby is gainir popularity in Japan.

Photographer:

Steve McCurry

● *Left*

Michi Shibuya, 60, of Asahi Village, Yamagata Prefecture.

Photographer:
Lynn Johnson

● *Above*

Daini Primary School students in Kamakura make sure they have a room with a view. Japanese schools do not normally employ cleaning staff. Teachers and pupils are expected to clean up after themselves.

Photographer:
Jay Maisel

● *Right*

The Kabuki-cho entertainme[nt]
district of Shinjuku, one of t[he]
busiest in Japan. The Yaman[ote]
line trains headed for Shinjuk[u]
Station are green, and the
Chuo-line trains are orange.
Japan has 46,362,000 regis-
tered motor vehicles, one fo[r]
every 20 meters (66 feet) of
paved road in the country.
Photographer:
Andy Levin

● *Right*

Mariko Rinbara on her way
to the Suzuki Violin School
in Tokyo. Enrolled at three
to four years of age, the
students use small-size instru-
ments. The founder of the
school, Shin'ichi Suzuki, based
his teaching system on the idea
that all children have innate
musical talent, which should
be developed before the age of
five.
Photographer:
Andrew Stawicki

● *Above*

Cartoons are favorite after-school fare for Hiroshima school children.

Photographer:
Stephanie Maze

● *Right*

Outside Osaka Castle.

Photographer:
Steve McCurry

● *Far right*

Kindergarten students exercise at Kita Osaka School.

Photographer:
Steve McCurry

● *Above, top*

Commuter train.

Photographer:
Arthur Grace

● *Above*

On the road again: even rock stars travel by train in Japan.

Photographer:
Alon Reininger

● *Right*

On the train between Aomori and Tokyo.

Photographer:
David Alan Harvey

● *Following page*

Mitsunobu Oshima and Tsutomu Muramatsu monitor the Osaka Prefectural Traffic Control System which links television cameras positioned throughout the city with traffic lights and signs. Since its installation in 1975, the system has reduced traffic deaths by 17 percent, accidents by 9.4 percent, travel time in Osaka by 17 percent, time at stop lights by 33 percent and exhaust gases by over one million kiloliters (over 35 million cubic feet) a year. The system cost ¥ 10 billion (US $40 million) to install, but according to the Osaka Prefectural Police, it has already saved drivers ¥ 211 billion (US $844 million) in time that can be devoted to economic activities.

Photographer:
Roger Ressmeyer

Roger Ressm

● *Above*

Outside Shibuya Station in
Tokyo.

Photographer:
Paul Chesley

● Above

● *Below*

In the control room of Fuji TV studios, Tokyo, during transmission of *Yuyake Nyan Nyan* ("Sunset Meow Meow"), a smash-hit variety show popular with pre-teens. Tokyo has seven television channels.

● *Right, top*

TV comedienne Toki Shiozawa in her trademark eyeglasses.

● *Right, middle*

"Let's Laugh." The theme of the show is that funny people have funny friends.

● *Right, bottom*

Stand-up comic Tamori (in glasses) gets a laugh with an imitation of a crazy foreigner. (Foreigners are often lampooned on Japanese television.) Sanma Akashiya, straight man from Osaka, applauds.

● *Left*

Inside job: Osaka Gas Company maintenance worker Noboru Kai inspects a gas tank. Midsummer temperatures inside reach 60°C (140°F).
Photographer:
Yoshio Hata

● *Above*

Outside job: early watermelons fetch premium prices. Shosuke Okabe offers these striped beauties from the southern island of Kyushu to customers in northern Honshu.
Photographer:
Jim Bryant

● *Left*

Rice seedlings are transplanted by hand in Iwate Prefecture. This is a back-breaking chore, and these days most rice seedlings in Japan are transplanted by machines.

Photographer:

Ian Lloyd

● *Above, top*

Covering the fields with polyethylene sheeting makes an early melon crop possible on the northern island of Hokkaido. Out of season fruit, sold as presents, fetches astronomical prices.

Photographer:

Leslie Smolan

● *Above*

Teruko Kawai waters a family garden in Nishiune.

Photographer:

Anne Day

Coal mining in Japan has a bitter history and an uncertain future. Less than a century ago, convicts were sent down into the mines where many died in mutinies and explosions. During World War II, the mines were kept going by prisoners of war and forced labor from Korea and China.

Until the 1950s, Japanese industry was mainly fueled by coal, and production reached a peak of 50 million tons a year. Then, the government converted most industries to imported oil. Coal mines were forcibly closed, leading to riots in the mining towns and a 282-day strike and lockout, modern Japan's longest and most bitter labor dispute. The miners were defeated, 120,000 of them lost their jobs and production was cut to 20 million tons a year.

Many people argue that Japan should get out of coal mining altogether. Even to maintain Japanese coal production at its current low level costs the treasury nearly ¥ 120 billion (US$500 million) yearly in subsidies to mine owners. Further, the volcanic structure of the main islands causes underground gas seepage, making Japanese coal mines among the most dangerous in the world.

In the spring of 1985, there were two more mining disasters in Japan. Eleven miners were killed by a blast in the 265-year-old Takashima Mine in Kyushu. Three weeks later, another 62 coal miners died in an explosion and fire in the Minami Oyubari Mine in Hokkaido. On June 7, American photographer Steve Krongard went to the site of the latest mining disaster, the grieving coal town of Yubari where 20 of the town's 22 mines have closed in the last two decades. The population of the living, once 100,000, is now under 40,000 and still falling.

● *Previous page*

A ghost town in the making. Mist shrouds Yubari, once famous for its productive, high-quality coal fields. Its mines have suffered many disasters whose victims lie in the cemetery above the town.

● *Left*

Children's *kendo* at the
Shudokan in Osaka. *Kendo*
is a form of Japanese fencing
adapted from the two-handed
samurai sword-fighting tech-
nique. The modern *kendo*
"sword" is made of bamboo.

Photographer:

Steve McCurry

● *Above, top and bottom*

A martial arts meet for senior
athletes is sponsored by the
Japan Welfare Association for
the Aged at Tokyo's Budokan,
the most famous indoor arena
in Japan.

Photographer:

Misha Erwitt

● *Left, top*

"Lucy Satan," a Filipina flamenco dancer at a theater in Koshigaya, Saitama Prefecture. Many hostesses and entertainers in Japan come from the Philippines. They often have visa problems.

Photographer:
Kazuyoshi Miyoshi

● *Below*

The rooftop garden of a Kob hotel.

Photographer:
Abbas

● *Previous page*

Play it again, Samurai: Bogey in Shinjuku, the first stop on the mountain route between the Shogun's capital, now Tokyo, and the Emperor's capital of Kyoto. It has been an entertainment center and red-light district for centuries. On June 7, 1985, nearly two million people passed through Shinjuku on their way to and from the Tokyo city center.

Photographer:
Bruno Barbey

● *Above*

Topless *sumo* at a rooftop beer garden in Tokyo. This match has not been recognized by the Japan Sumo Association, governing body of the sport.

Photographer:
Ethan Hoffman

E xcept for the snow-topped cone of Fuji, no image evokes Japan more powerfully to Westerners than the blank-white face of the *geisha.* But most foreigners—and these days, even some Japanese—are unclear about what *geisha* actually do.

In Japanese, the word means "artist" or "person of talent." The *Kodansha Encyclopedia of Japan* defines *geisha* as "women entertainers of a traditional type, who provide singing, dancing, conversation, games and companionship to customers." We can add that *geisha* do most of their entertaining at parties that (apart from the *geisha*) are exclusively male, where a great deal of beer, *sake* and whiskey are consumed and where everyone has a jolly, drunken time. (If not, the *geisha* are not doing their job properly.)

Are *geisha,* then, a sort of Japanese party girl? Not exactly. The average age is 40-plus, and one is still in business in Tokyo at the age of 82. Nevertheless, the theme of their games, conversation, singing and dancing is, most of the time, one way or another, sex. They play, it is true, the *shamisen,* an instrument rather like a ukulele and not much more difficult to learn, and they sing traditional folk songs and perform intricate dances. Their real skills, however, are flirting with men, making them laugh at suggestive games, persuading them to drink and generally making sure the party goes swimmingly.

This sounds rather like the role of a Western society hostess, and in many ways it is. But Japanese women over the centuries have not been encouraged to develop social skills. Hence, the appearance of a special kind of courtesan and entertainer trained to attend at male parties, for substantial pay, and therefore, exclusively for rich or powerful men.

Some *geisha* develop long-term relationships with their clients, learn about their business affairs and offer advice on the stock market and such.

There are probably less than a thousand of these high-class *geisha* left in all Japan. (A century ago, there were at least 80,000 of them.) But lower down the market, there are still some 15,000 *onsen geisha* who entertain at the equivalent of office parties at hot-spring resorts. These are less refined affairs. Finally, Japan has no less than 250,000 bar hostesses who offer male customers the same kind of companionship, flattery, relaxed atmosphere and flirtation the *geisha* used to do, minus the expensive *kimono* and heavy "flower fees." (Since it would be unseemly for the *geisha* to speak of money, she requests her hourly fee in flowers which normally represent ¥ 10,000 or US $40 apiece.)

To get down to basic misconceptions, *geisha*, then, are not prostitutes, although they did start off as entertainers in brothels (illegal in Japan since 1958).

● *eft, bottom*

hisuzu, at home, hears her
edule for the evening.
ographer:
i **Cobb**

● *Below*

Kimisuzu returns from an
assignment by hired car. In
both Kyoto and Tokyo, a few
geisha still travel to work by
rickshaw, the last people in
Japan to do so.
Photographer:
Jodi Cobb

● *Right*

Kimisuzu goes off to work.
Photographer:
Jodi Cobb

Some have love affairs with selected clients, and some have married rich businessmen and politicians. The *mizuage*, or first sexual experience of a young *geisha*, traditionally commanded the highest fee.

Young women like Kimisuzu (19), depicted in this essay, enter the profession as apprentices, called *maiko* or "dance child" in the city of Kyoto, where the classic tradition is strongest. Even here, however, *geisha* are rapidly becoming curators of a museum art. Japanese feminists hate the whole idea, and many young Japanese women who once would have become *geisha* find the arduous years of training and the prospect of a career entertaining boozed-up men unappealing.

A pattern of more comradely relations between the sexes is emerging in Japan. But progress is slow, and in some form or another, the accomplished courtesan, that is, the professional drinking companion, confidante and (if the price is right) conquest still has an assured place in Japan for a long time to come.

Left, bottom

imisuzu works at an open-air
nner party by the bank of
e Kamo River in Kyoto.
he other two women in at-
ndance are waitresses. *Geisha*
 not bring food to the table,
t they are responsible for
uring the drinks.

otographer:
di Cobb

● *Below*

Kimisuzu keeps her diary
while Michael Jackson keeps
watch.

Photographer:
Jodi Cobb

● *Right*

A *geisha* needs help to remove
her elaborate make-up.

Photographer:
Jodi Cobb

Chiyonofuji, 30, one of the two current *sumo* grand champions, has his hair dressed by an apprentice—a privilege of championship rank. Chiyonofuji (born Mitsugu Akimoto) has been wrestling since 1973, is married and has one daughter. At 120 kilograms (264 pounds), the muscular Chiyonofuji was hailed as the forerunner of a trend toward slimmer, more willowy *sumo* wrestlers who relied on strength rather than pure bulk. But in June 1985, the success of Samoan man-mountain Konishiki (Salevaa Artisanoe), who strains the scales at 225 kilograms (496 pounds), had proponents of the new concept blubbering.

Photographer:
Mark S. Wexler

● *Right*

Brothers measuring up.
Photography Contest Winner:
Kunio Watabiki

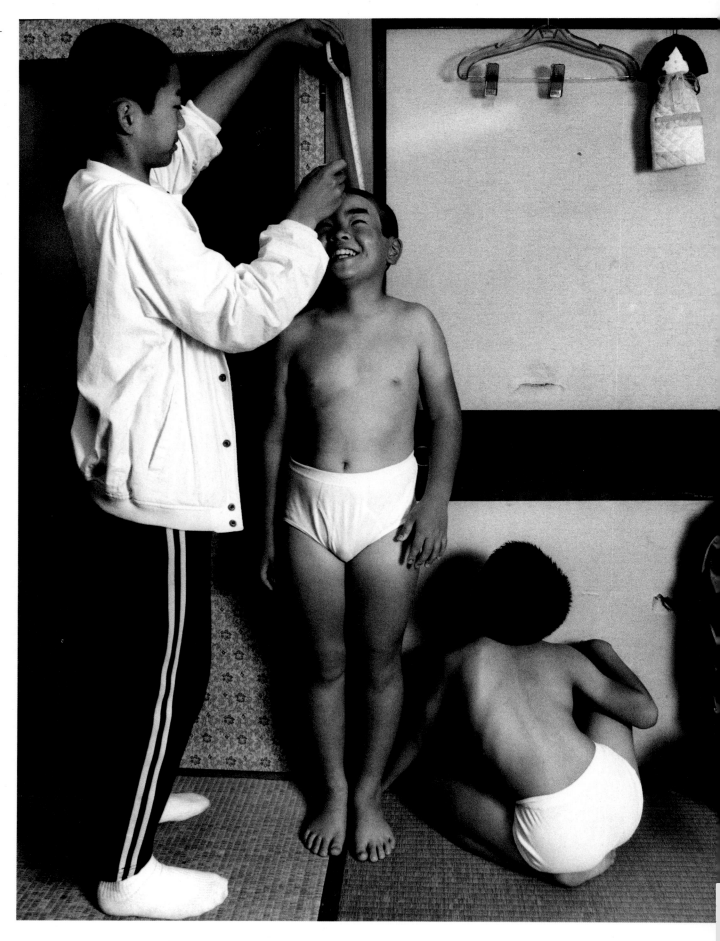

● *Below*

The Ikeda High School base-ball team—considered one of Japan's best in 1985—bowing at the end of a training session as an expression of gratitude for the use of their diamond. High-school players practice four or five hours every day.
Photographer:
Ethan Hoffman

● *Below, bottom*

Sadaharu Oh, Japan's Babe Ruth and now manager of the Yomiuri Giants.
Photographer:
Shelly Katz

● *Right*

On June 7, 1985, the Chunicl Dragons shut out the Yomiur Giants 2 to 0. Baseball is the most popular imported sport in Japan. First played at Toky University in 1873, it is no longer thought of as foreign, and most Japanese call it *yaky* or "field ball."
Photographer:
Shelly Katz

● *Right and below*

Pachinko is the Japanese national obsession. More than 70 percent of Japanese men and 30 percent of the women play regularly. No one else in the world plays it (except Japanese-Americans in Hawaii). Winning involves a little skill and a lot of luck. Machines pay off in a torrent of steel balls, which are traded for chocolates, cigarettes, canned food and similar low-value prizes. These can usually (and illegally) be further traded for cash. Japan has professional

pachinko players, *pachinko* magazines and *pachinko* widows. It has been estimated that ¥4.5 trillion (US$18 billion) pass through the machines each year. Rafael Gaillarde, who studied the game in Sapporo, reported, "Je l'avais trouvé fascinant. Le *pachinko* est une espèce de méditation méchanisée."

Photographers, clockwise from right:
Rafael Gaillarde
Rafael Gaillarde
Steve McCurry

Previous page

ne hundred sardine boats put sea from Maisaka, Shizuoka efecture.

otograpy Contest Winner:

itsuru Yamauchi

● *Left*

The fiberglass Statue of Liberty atop Tokyo's Hotel New York plainly signals that it is a love hotel.

Photographer:

Mark S. Wexler

● *Above*

Many countries have hotels that rent rooms by the hour for purposes other than sleeping, but in Japan "love hotels" openly proclaim their function and advertise regularly on television.

Originally seedy back-street operations, Japanese love hotels have become a bizarre folk art. From the outside, they look like Moorish castles, European cathedrals, futuristic space stations, ocean liners—anything but regular hotels. Inside they are fantasy palaces with medieval rooms complete with suits of armor, jungle settings where clients can go ape in borrowed gorilla suits, boats surrounded by artificial ocean for shipboard romances and beds shaped like luxury automobiles, conch shells, Queen Elizabeth's coronation coach and just about anything else. The beds oscillate, rock, roll and rotate, and many are equipped with closed-circuit television cameras to record the proceedings. The space-shuttle bed above at the Super Fashion Hotel in Osaka moves down the launching rail automatically when a concealed microphone detects sighs and moans.

Studies indicate that most love hotel clients are married— to each other. They patronize love hotels because of crowded conditions at home, inquisitive children and, as the TV advertisements promise, to put some glamour back into their mar-

riages. Nevertheless, guests' cars have their license plates covered, room keys drop from faceless automated dispensers and every effort is made to preserve secrecy. Love hotels have become so popular that travelers who just want a night's rest are sometimes compelled to sleep under mirrored ceilings on waterbeds which produce a light surf if the wrong button is touched accidently.

Photographer:

Roger Ressmeyer

● *Left, top*

This *yakitori* (grilled chicken) snack bar in Saitama Prefecture has been in business 30 years. The best *yakitori* is roasted over charcoal. The fan is to keep the charcoal glowing.

Photography Contest Winner:
Nobuyuki Kobayashi

● *Left, bottom*

These revelers missed the last train from Shinjuku Station. Very likely, they were at work bright and early the next day.

Photographer:
Bruno Barbey

● *Below*

This capsule hotel in Osaka rents roomlets by the night ¥ 3,000 (US$12). Originally built in the entertainment district of Osaka for people who missed the last train home, capsule hotels now provide mini-accommodation for all sorts of people around Japan. They are strictly for one person.

Photographer:
Roger Ressmeyer

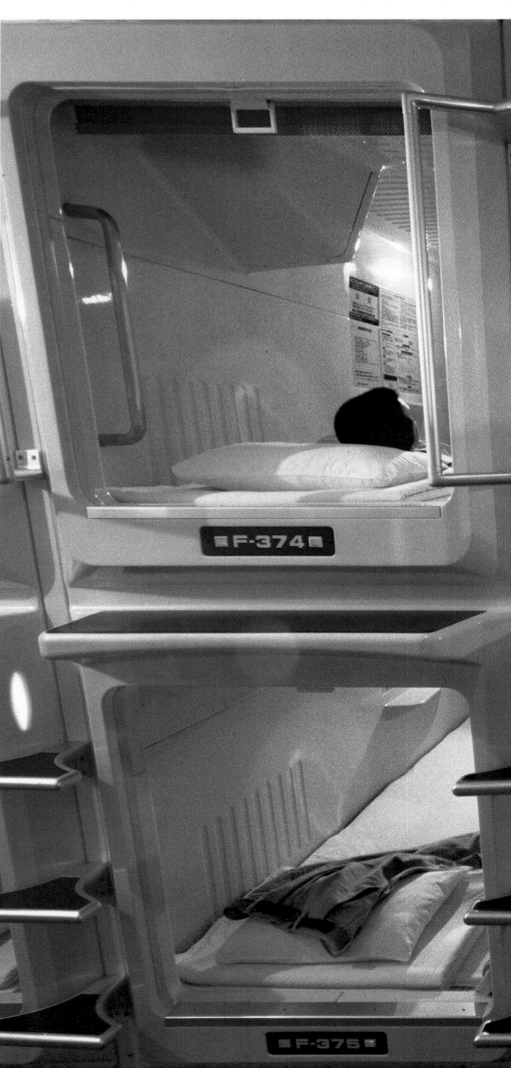

In a recent survey of the Japanese people, 62 percent of respondents gave their favorite recreation as sleeping. Here are the world's most industrious people hard at their favorite pastime on June 7, 1985: (clockwise from the right) in the "Dunkin' Donuts" at Shinjuku Station in Tokyo, at an ice-cream truck in Hachinohe City, aboard a ferry crossing the Inland Sea from Honshu to Shikoku, under a Tokyo billboard advertising the latest Akira Kurosawa movie, *Ran*, and on a Tokyo subway train.
Photographers, clockwise from the right:
Andy Levin
Jim Bryant
Masanori Kobayashi
Paul Chesley
Tadanori Saito

● *Far left*

Tokyo night life as seen at the Tsubaki House Discotheque on June 7, 1985.

Photographer:
Gerd Ludwig

● *Left*

Mr. Yamashita dances with one of the *onsen geisha* entertaining at his retirement party. A colleague provides the music by singing along with a *karaoke* ("empty-orchestra") tape. Guests at *onsen* (hot spring resorts) customarily change into light cotton *yukata* or robes on arrival.

Photographer:
Bob Davis

● *Above*

Watching the latest science-fiction movie special effects at "SFX Academy '85," a week-long exhibit at the La Foret Museum in trendy Harajuku, Tokyo.

Photographer:
Torin Boyd

Staggering home from a night on the town in Shinjuku, Tokyo. Public drunkenness is not a crime in Japan. In fact, heavy drinking plays an important role as a social lubricant. Not only are business deals set up over drinks, but when the *sake* flows, Japanese reserve often gives way to maudlin sentimentality and instant friendship. Employees may argue with their bosses, confident that all will be forgotten the next day.

Photographer:
Arnaud de Wildenberg

● *Above, top*

The Erina Bar in Tokushima is too small to have a band. Patrons come to sing along with the *kara-oke* ("empty orchestra") tapes at left.

Photographer:
Robin Moyer

● *Above*

Kinki gourmets: patrons of a hot-spring resort in the Kinki district enjoy their *sushi* in the raw.

Photographer:
Yoshiaki Nagashima

Left

rotenburo or open-air bath at
e Takami Hotel in Atagawa.
tographer:
egory Heisler

11:30 PM

● *Left*

I hear music but there's no
guitar. Strumming the air at a
Nara disco.
Photographer:
Hiroshi Hamaya

● *Left*

Members of a nearby agri-
cultural cooperative enjoy a
weekend party at a hot spring
in Matsuyama City.
Photographer:
Masanori Kobayashi

● *Left*

End of the day: squid boats off the Izu Peninsula, near Tokyo. Fishing boats burn brilliant lamps to attract squid, and when astronauts orbit the Earth, they see the whole of Japan traced in light. Individually, squid boats cast a fairly bright glow. Together, they make the brightest light on Earth.

Photographer:

Gregory Heisler

● *Above*

Yakitori, grilled chunks of chicken on a stick, are most often eaten as snacks.

Photographer:

Andy Levin

● *Following page*

Tokyo, looking east from the top of the Sumitomo Sankaku building in Shinjuku.

Photographer:

Graeme Outerbridge

Photographers' Assignment Locations

Hagi City, Yamaguchi-Ken

Hokkaido

1 Rishiri
Wilbur E. Garrett

2 Asahikawa
Diego Goldberg

3 Teshikaga-cho
Jack Corn

4 Sapporo
Rafael Gaillarde

5 Yubari
Tsuneo Enari
Steve Krongard

6 Kushiro
Jennifer Erwitt
Kent Kobersteen

7 Niikappu
David Alan Harvey

Honshu

8 Tsugaru
Masatoshi Naito

9 Morioka
Ian Lloyd

10 Fukuura
Lynn Johnson

11 Sendai
Tom Skudra

12 Niigata
Alon Reininger

13 Sado Island
Masahisa Fukase

14 Fukushima
Rich Clarkson

15 Nikko
Kazuyoshi Nomachi

16 Tsukuba
Bohn-Chang Koo

17 Narita
Julio Donoso

18 Kujukuri
Aaron Chang

19 Chiba
Ikko Narahara
Hiroyuki Matsumoto
Munesuke Yamamoto

20 Ichikawa
Arnaud de Wildenberg

21 Tokyo
Ellen Bailey
Bruno Barbey
Lucy Birmingham
Torin Boyd
David Burnett
Gary Chapman
Paul Chesley
Misha Erwitt
Arthur Grace
Tom Haley
Pauline Johnson
Hiroji Kubota
Kaku Kurita
Andy Levin
Gerd Ludwig
Leonard Lueras
Masaaki Miyazawa
Kazuyoshi Miyoshi
Graeme Outerbridge
Bill Pierce
Bill Simpkins
Neal Slavin
Rick Smolan
Andrew Stawicki
Kiyomi Takeyama
Junichi Tanabe
Neal Ulevich
Mark S. Wexler
Joy Wolf
Haruyoshi Yamaguchi

22 Urayasu
Dilip Mehta

23 Kawasaki
Jyoji Hashiguchi

24 Yokohama
Jon Pite

25 Asaka
Nicole Bengiveno

26 Kamakura
Jay Maisel

27 Aikawa
Eddie Adams

28 Atami
Bob Davis

29 Mount Fuji
Victor Fisher

30 Shizuoka
Katsumi Kasahara
Jean-Pierre Laffont

31 Matsumoto
Al Harvey

32 Nagano
Toshi Matsumoto

33 Tateyama
Galen Rowell

34 Toyama
Gregory Heisler

35 Kanazawa
Michael Melford

36 Fukui
Yoshiaki Nagashima

37 Nagoya
Shelly Katz

38 Kyoto
Jose Azel
Jodi Cobb
Nicholas Devore
Matthew Naythons

39 Nara
Hiroshi Hamaya

40 Osaka
Steve McCurry
Roger Ressmeyer
Issei Suda

41 Kobe
Abbas

42 Tottori
Maddy Miller

43 Okayama
Anne Day

44 Matsue
Stephanie Maze

45 Etajima Island
P. F. Bentley

46 Hiroshima
Eikoh Hosoe
Rudi Meisel

47 Hagi
James Nachtwey

Shikoku

48 Tokushima
Ethan Hoffman
Robin Moyer

49 Kochi
Masanori Kobayashi

50 Matsuyama
Dan Dry

Kyushu

51 Hita
Adam Jahiel

52 Fukuoka
Cliff Hollenbeck
Jun Miki

53 Nagasaki
Shomei Tomatsu

54 Minamata
Shisei Kuwabara

55 Ibusuki
Mike Yamashita

Ryukyu Islands

56 Okinawa
Greg Davis
David Doubilet
Takeji Iwamiya
Eli Reed

Asaka, near Tokyo

Kyushu

Sado, Niigata

Ryukyu Islands

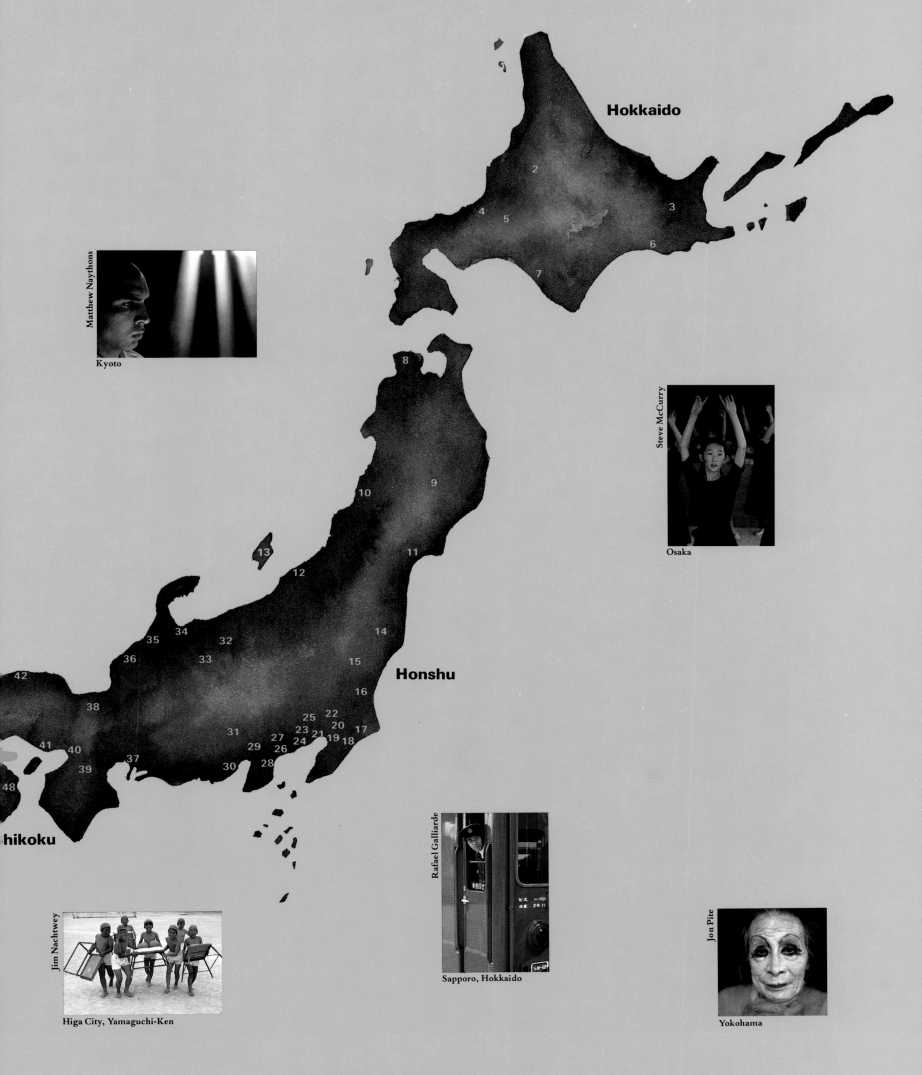

Hokkaido

2

3

4
5

6

7

Matthew Naythons

Matthew Naythons
Kyoto

8

Steve McCurry

9

10

11

Osaka

13

12

14

34
35

32

Honshu

36

33

42

15

16

38

22
25 20
23 21   17
27 19
24
29 26 18

41
40

31

37
39

28
30

48

hikoku

Rafael Galliarde

Jim Nachtwey

Sapporo, Hokkaido

Jon Pite

Higa City, Yamaguchi-Ken

Yokohama

Andy Levin

Tokyo

227

A Day in the Life Revisited

"Say cheezu": Neal Slavin took the official *A Day in the Life of Japan* group portrait outside the Imperial Palace in Tokyo.

Gerd Ludwig

I had an idea of what Japan would be like before I came, but by the end of the assignment the Japanese mentality seemed even more foreign to me than before. It's a complete secret to me. The longer I stay here, the more confused I get.

Dan Dry

I think this project was particularly fun because none of us knew what we were doing including David and Rick.

Ian Lloyd

I woke up at 12:02, two minutes into the day, and wondered why I was awake. I didn't have to get up until 3 a.m. I looked at my watch and thought, "Aha, this is the collective unconscious of 100 photographers rousing me from my sleep saying, "Get up, boy. It's time to shoot."

Bill Pierce

I hate the Japanese bureaucracy. It absolutely drives me out of my mind. The amazing thing is that once you begin to reach them as people, as individuals, the same people who were putting up all the roadblocks turn out to be the most incredibly decent, good, thoughtful, kind, enthusiastic, super people in the world.

n April 14, 1985, *A Day in the Life of Japan* pulled up to the curb outside the international departures terminal at New York's Kennedy Airport—riding in a rented station wagon and a stretch Cadillac. At the time, that was it: 47 pieces of baggage, computers, typewriters, books, assorted stationary and half a dozen hastily assembled staffers with co-director David Cohen in command. The destination tags read ''Narita'', Tokyo's sprawling international airport. The other co-director, Rick Smolan, was already in Japan. Momentous words were spoken as the plane lifted off, but due to the effects of the champagne that followed, no one seems to remember what they were.

At some point, someone has probably tried to import something into Japan that was odder than the chaotic multi-million dollar travelling photo expedition and mobile publishing house that comprises the *Day in the Life* project. The American marketing whiz who once tried to sell cake mix in a country where no one has an oven comes to mind. The early betting on *A Day in the Life of Japan* was not much better. "It's a closed society that will never understand what you're doing and besides no one there speaks English." That was the instant response from practically everyone, including me. I was sitting in my office on Madison Avenue when I heard that Rick and David had about six weeks to track down one hundred of the hardest to find photographers in the world, get them all to Tokyo at the same time and then spread them across Japan on well researched assignments. They had a week to edit a hundred thousand or so pictures. And then a leisurely five weeks to get an impeccably designed and written, 300-page, large format book to the printers—in English and Japanese editions. Obviously, it couldn't work.

What you have in your hands is convincing evidence that it did. But there was, undoubtedly, a degree of morbid curiosity among those of us who decided to

cancel assignments in Hollywood or begged some time off from the midtown Manhattan news factories to watch Rick and David go over the falls—or down Mt. Fuji, as it were—in a barrel. It certainly wasn't the salary.

I first met Rick Smolan in Hong Kong in 1978, where he beat me by a wide margin for the title of longest hair in the *Time-Life* news bureau. At the time, Rick was commuting between Hong Kong and Australia where he was shooting a National Geographic cover story about a young lady who trekked alone by camel 3,000 miles across the continent's dead heart. He was smitten with the place. Australia, he once told me, was the only place where you could spend an entire day with a pleasant group of people and never once be asked what you did for a living. Rick was, in fact, having some doubts about the whole business of being a magazine gypsy. Shortly thereafter, he turned amateur publisher, and *A Day in the Life of Australia* was shakily on its way.

There are two dozen publishers of any note in Australia, and every one of them turned the idea down flat. The book, shot on March 1,1981 by a crew of one hundred photographers, and self-published by Rick and a few friends in Sydney, became an astonishing success, selling 200,000 copies around the world. One of its many midwives was a hustling young Yalie named David Cohen, then managing director of a New York photo agency. Cohen came to Australia to help out for a month and never quite returned to his old job.

Despite the book's success and Rick's oath of, ''never again,'' he and David frantically organized *A Day in the Life of Hawaii* (December 2, 1983). They both said, ''never again,'' again and then immediately launched into *A Day in the Life of Canada* (June 8, 1984), another all-time national best seller. After Canada, ''never'' lasted nearly nine months. Rick and David were in Mexico when the telephone rang: Jim Boff, American Express, Tokyo, calling out of the blue. It seems Jim Firestone was about to be named President of American Express, Japan. He had seen a copy of the Canada book (Amex's Toronto branch had sponsored a travelling *Day in the Life of Canada* photography exhibit.) Had Smolan and Cohen ever thought about doing *A Day in the Life of Japan?* As a matter of fact they had, quickly crossing it off as impractical. Still, three days later, Rick (who lost the coin toss) was on a plane to Tokyo with one pair of jeans and three shirts. As things turned out, he didn't make it back home to New York for four months.

By normal publishing standards, *Day in the Life* books are extraordinarily expensive to produce. *A Day in the Life of Japan*, for instance, worked with an overall budget of just under ¥ 850,000,000, roughly $3,500,000. (The largest single sum goes for the world's best four-color printing in Japan). Bookstore sales could never cover those kinds of costs. Magazines solve the problem by selling advertising. *Day in the Life* books do it with sponsors —companies that want to generate good will in the community. Some corporations provide money, others provide services, either free or at greatly reduced cost. The one condition—and everyone understands this—is no strings attached.

Well, almost. American Express offered their support with one proviso: the book, whatever was in it, had to be on the shelves in time for the Christmas book-buying season—one aspect of Christianity that means nearly as much in gift-mad Japan as it does in North America. Working backward through the fastest possible schedule for shipping, printing, color separations, layout and editing, that meant a shoot date no later than the first week in June, more or less exactly when Japan's funereal rainy season reaches Tokyo. Rick and David, after talking it over on the phone, took the proverbial deep breath and gave American Express a "yes".

That set in motion a process that has been compared (by Rick) to frantically building a glider on the back of a flatbed truck that is hurtling out of control toward the edge of a cliff. The situation was, as any Japanese business-man or bureaucrat says when faced with an unreasonable

request, *choto ne*— literally "a little" (as in, a little difficult) and actually meaning "highly unlikely" verging on "impossible". It was a phrase we heard often.

But not, happily enough, from the photographers. "Our peers, our heroes and the best of the next generation" is Rick's standard phrase for who gets invited to *Day in the Life* projects; which in this case meant 130 men and women representing a fair slice of the best working photographers and picture editors in the world. Like the staffers, very few photographers accept the invitation for the money or the multitudinous goodies and freebies organized by production manager, Jennifer Erwitt. They seem to relish the element of competition, though it is considered very poor form to say so. And one or two will admit that they actually enjoy what amounts to a cross between a very large, rather exotic party and an annual convention.

One nice thing, of course, is that someone else does most of the drudge work: little things like booking a hundred-odd round-trip air tickets, arranging a thousand-odd hotel room-nights, cooking up challenging assignments the length and breadth of Japan and providing the cars, train and plane tickets, contacts and interpreters. And while all that is going on, digging up enough money to pay for the whole business.

Just locating all the honorable invitees is tough enough. Some are not much more difficult to find than a guy who rides the 5 o'clock train home each night after a hard day at the bank. Others are self-avowed homeless, globe-trotting rogues and it takes sixteen telephone calls and telexes across eight time zones, three languages and a dozen addresses to deliver a two-line message. Multiply that by 130, as our logistics coordinator Victor Fisher had to do, then try to find out where they think they'll be on May 31st and where they'd like their air tickets sent

David Cohen

I was travelling on a commuter train from Tokyo out to a small suburb called Shibamata. I did like the Japanese do and put my camera bag on one of the overhead racks. When I got off to change trains at a small station seven stops out of town, I realized that I had left my camera bag with my wallet in it on the rack. In a small panic, I went to the stationmaster's office—a tiny, old fashioned but fastidiously neat shed built on a platform next to the tracks. I explained my problem through an interpreter. The stationmaster asked a series of questions: How long ago did the train leave you here? Was your car near the front or back of the train? Was the rack near the front or back of the car? What color was the bag?

Then he consulted his big old schedule book, made a single phone call, and asked us to wait for five minutes. Three minutes later the phone rang. My bag had been located, and it was returned to me in forty minutes.

The Tokyo commuter lines move ten million people a day on thousands of trains through hundreds of stations and it took them precisely three minutes to find my bag. It had nothing to do with computers and the vaunted Japanese technology—the stationmaster's hut was straight out of a 1940's movie. It had everything to do with the stationmaster's supreme confidence that every train in the system would be exactly where it was supposed to be when it was supposed to be there. This was backed up by a firm faith that none of JNR's respected commuters would touch a camerabag that didn't belong to him.

The Occident meets the Orient: Two generations of photographers, Jennifer Erwitt and Hiroshi Hamaya, strolled through Hamaya's home town of Oiso.

Hands across the sea: Project co-director David Cohen negotiates with a potential sponsor in Shinjuku, Tokyo.

Always on hand: Writer Murray Sayle awaited the muse.

Pressing ahead: Publicity Director Patti Richards plays matchmaker between photographers and NHK video teams.

Roll reversal: Project co-director Rick Smolan poses for young photographers at the Kodak children's workshop held at the roof garden of My City department store in Tokyo.

Paul Chesley

A la moat: Arnaud de Wildenberg of Paris and Gregory Heisler of New York did an impromptu ballet outside the Imperial Palace.

Steve McCurry

Torin Boyd

In the bag: Photographer Jay Maisel (left) chomped on one of his trademark cigars, as a future photographer (above) trie[d] out his new camera at the Koda[k] children's workshop in Shinjuku Tokyo.

and you get the idea. One photographer really was in Timbuktu, and for all we could ever figure out, still is.

One problem at least was handled with nearly unbelievable aplomb: finding space for a temporary headquarters amidst some of the costliest real estate on earth. Shortly after the project went "go," Rick stopped by the Tokyo office of Apple Computer, hoping to borrow a Macintosh computer ("I'm helpless without one") until his own could be sent from New York with his clothes. Fred Scherrer, newly arrived as Apple Japan's national sales manager, was happy to oblige. He liked the *Day in the Life* idea and offered Rick and company a spacious war room in Apple's high-tech Akasaka office. He said, "I wanted to give our Japanese colleagues a chance to see how Americans operate."

Soon, the Tokyo *Day in the Life* office bore a passing (and thoroughly misleading) resemblance to its Japanese equivalent: a partitionless room full of desks, constantly ringing telephones and wandering workers. At best, that guaranteed a kind of rough democracy in which everyone helped each other and very few secrets were kept. At worst, the background noise and general chaos convinced potential sponsors and key government officials solicited by telephone that *A Day in the Life of Japan* was operated from a bank of phone booths in Tokyo Station.

Fred Scherrer's hopes notwithstanding, most of Apple's Japanese colleagues regarded us as slightly dangerous. *Day in the Life's* own Japanese staff faced a day at the office with alternating amusement and utter disbelief. Yuko Katsumura, Kiyomi Takeyama and Munesuke Yamamoto had the bad luck to be the only ones in an office of twenty people who could accomplish such feats as, say, using a phone book or giving an address to a cab driver. They also tried, more or less futilely, to teach us something approaching decent Japanese manners. By the middle of May, Katsumura-san could translate two simultaneous conversations, while politely stalling a third on the telephone.

Not surprisingly, many potential Japanese sponsors failed to view all this chaos as evidence of American creativity at work. And even with American Express backing, a lot of funds still had to be raised. The financial going was tough for a while, but one by one breakthroughs were made. While still in New York, David had made a day trip to Rochester, where a meeting with Eastman Kodak vice

president Ray DeMoulin, produced a deal for badly needed cash and 4,000 rolls of film plus processing. In Tokyo, Japan Air Lines, with public relations whiz Geoff Tudor running interference, came through with round trip air tickets for everyone involved. Richard Handl put out the welcome mat at the towering new Hilton International hotel in Shinjuku. And Olympus Camera stole a march on its numerous hometown rivals, by opening a professional service suite and providing its latest model auto-everything camera for each photographer.

That still left, of course, the small problem of coming up with the ideas that became the assignments that became the photographs that fill *A Day in the Life of Japan*. Everyone pitched in, including the photographers, who were asked via questionnaire if there was anything special they wanted to shoot. Most left it to us, but if the rest had had their way this book could have been titled *A Day in the Life of Thatched-Roof Farm Houses, Geisha and Ancient Buddhist Temples.*

Rick and David had something a little different in mind, and called on two esteemed and well informed gentlemen of Japan. Hiroshi Hamaya, a revered Japanese photographer and Murray Sayle, an expatriate Australian journalist, gave the assignments more bite. The list of ideas produced by each would have been enough for *A Year in the Life.* The assignment team—Jane Condon, Neil Gross, Arnold Drapkin, Anne Day, Jenny Sayle, Pauline Johnson, Yutaka Suzuki, Mune Yamamoto and myself—faced the problem of winnowing the ideas down, pulling them into focus and hassling the eight million details which comprised the practicalities of who, where and how. We even added a few assignment ideas of our own.

For the better part of a month, everyone worked around the clock. Neil, Jane and Jenny repeatedly called on contacts built up over years of living and working in Tokyo. By the rules of *giri*, they now owe most of Japan favors for the rest of their lives. The Foreign Press Center of Japan, in the shape of Ishikawa-san, backed us up in our dealings with the awe-inspiring Japanese bureaucracy. For reasons that remain obscure (but for which we will be forever grateful), the high powered Japan External Trade Organization (JETRO) put the resources of two dozen offices around the country at our disposal.

For finesse, confidence and sheer throw-weight, however, nothing could match Nippon Hoso Kyokai, the massive Japanese broadcasting organization known as NHK. Shortly after *A Day in the Life of Japan*'s official press launch, Mr. Nishizawa, NHK's special chief cameraman, telephoned publicity director Patti Richards to ask if the network might make a film about the project. What sort? Say, a one hour documentary, for nationwide, prime-time broadcast in early July. Which photographers did they want to cover? All of them, of course. And for the benefit of those that found that unbelievable, (in fact, NHK has 350 camera crews in Japan) they started the next day by stationing a cameraman, soundman and field producer, full time, in the *Day in the Life* offices.

NHK's involvement turned what might have been a minor feature story into a major media event. Every TV network in Japan figured that if NHK was covering *Day in the Life* so heavily, there must be something important going on, and the newspapers figured that if all the networks were covering it. . . .) One group of photographers arriving at Narita airport for the shoot was greeted by a phalanx of camera crews and reporters who completely ignored Donald Sutherland, Jennifer O'Neil and a baffled group of American movie stars arriving on the same flight to attend the Tokyo Film Festival. As word got around, international networks including CBS, CNN and the Canadian Broadcasting Corporation jumped in, setting off a series of heated tug-of-wars over who got exclusive rights to which photographers. In the end, NHK deployed 65 camera crews to shoot more than 900 hours of videotape.

Having a television crew in tow on shoot day made it unlikely that any of the photographers would get stranded, arrested or lost, and in fact none did—a first for *Day in the Life* . Armed with plane, train and ferry tickets, Nissan rental cars, special press passes, assignment sheets, what looked like twelve tons of equipment and some stern words from Jane Condon and Murray Sayle about appropriate decorum, the photographers spread out across Japan on the morning of Wednesday, June 5. That and the next day were scheduled for scouting and in some cases, for chucking hopelessly bizarre, unworkable or stunningly boring assignments. There were mercifully few of those.

What came back were 135,000 extraordinary images of Japan, as the *Day in the Life* phrase goes, taken during a single ordinary day. It took seven days from the time the first processed film reached the office for the crew of assembled picture editors, working 15 hours a day on 10 light tables, to reduce that overwhelming pile of slides and negatives to a manageable number of selected photographs. Hand carried back to New York, these were printed as 8 by 10 inch glossies, studied, argued over, horse traded and finally laid out in final form by a design team headed by Leslie Smolan of Carbone Smolan Associates. On July 20th, less than seven weeks from the shoot day, the essentially finished book, including text and captions by Murray Sayle, arrived back in Japan at Toppan's printing plant outside Tokyo.

People say it might be the best *Day in the Life* book yet. It's not surprising, given the size and diversity of Japan. More people pass through Tokyo's Shinjuku Station each morning than live in all the Hawaiian Islands. Neither Australia nor Canada can match the population of even metropolitan Tokyo. Each of these projects, to be sure, involved a vast amount of luck, and this one was no exception. A friend of a friend turns up Koko Kato, who marshals a small army of enthusiastic volunteer interpreters (and gets our vote as Japan's first woman Prime Minister). *Day in the Life* intern Tory Boyd finds himself sitting at a table at a nightclub with Julian Lennon. The summer rains start in Tokyo on June 8th, a week behind schedule, and then it rains all over Japan as it hasn't rained for 30 years.

But the truth is that it probably would have worked rain or shine. At the worst moment in the week before June 7th, someone floated a fail-safe plan: buy a hundred train tickets to every part of Japan and let the photographers pick them out of a box at random and simply go. You could do that with Japan and our photographers. The trains go everywhere, and those behind the camera could make vivid, compelling pictures in a parking garage. That's the strange thing about *Day in the Life* projects. They're impossible and inevitable at the same time.

—Spencer Reiss

Abbas
I was assigned to photograph the Japanese mafia, the yakusa. I was fascinated by their extremes of tenderness and violence. When I arrived at their headquarters, it wasn't like going into a mafia headquarters, it was like walking into a college girl's dormitory. They were all very shy and retired, didn't know what to say and were reluctant to let me photograph them. Through my translator, I tried to explain that I was from Paris and that I worked for Magnum. One really tough gangster looked up and said, ''Oh yes, that's the agency Robert Capa was with.'' It was incredible that this guy knew about Magnum and Capa. Once they heard that I covered wars and was with Magnum they let me photograph them.
The organization in the headquarters itself stunned me. It looked like a normal business office with people on the telephone but there was a TV monitor to check the streets in case of attack and a big board with names on it. They said, ''This is how we keep track of our members, which ones are in or out of prison, the ones about to go to prison, and the ones about to be paroled.''

Steve Krongard
A Day in the Life of Japan became a sort of media event and this made it a little hard to shoot sometimes. On the morning of the shoot, my translator and I were walking through the village and, of course, we had our NHK television crew with us. Soon I noticed a taxi following us. The taxi stopped and a reporter jumped out with a camera. Then a little van pulled up and a Sapporo TV crew climbed out, then two more newspaper reporters showed up, and I started to feel like the pied piper. Here I am trying to get some candid shots in this quiet Hokkaido village with the assembled media of Japan following five steps back.

Jean-Pierre Laffont

Maddy Miller

Rick Smolan

Star search: Steve Krongard made his Japanese television debut .

Castaway: Jean-Pierre Laffont of Sygma Photos broke his ankle while shooting publicity stills for a pirate movie. He photographed the Shizuoka Saiseikei Hospital from a wheelchair.

Wing and a prayer: Assignment coordinator Yuko Katsumura made her first helicopter flight.

Photographers' Biographies

Abbas

A Day in the Life of Hawaii 1983

Abbas
Iranian/Paris
A Third Worlder transplanted to the West, Abbas has covered Asia, Africa, the Middle East and South America during the past 15 years. His work has appeared in many major magazines, and currently he is working on a long-term project on Mexico. He is a member of the Magnum Photo Agency.

Eddie Adams

Saigon 1969

Eddie Adams
American/New York, New York
Winner of the Pulitzer Prize and the Silver Prix Award of the Advertising Association of Japan, Adams is one of the most decorated and published photographers in America with over 500 awards to his credit. He has photographed leaders in all fields, from the heads of state to the superstars of film, sports and high fashion. His work appears in prestigious magazines and newspapers around the world.

José Azel
Cuban/New York, New York
Before moving to New York in 1982, Azel was a staff photographer with the *Miami Herald*. He is currently a regular contributor to Contact Press Images and has covered the 1984 Summer Olympics, Pope John Paul II's South American visit and the 1984 Democratic and Republican conventions.

Ellen Bailey
American/New York, New York
Originally from Kentucky, Bailey began her career as a rock and roll photographer. Her work has appeared in several San Francisco galleries. She plans to do more corporate and editorial photography in the future.

Bruno Barbey
French/Paris
A member of Magnum Photo Agency since 1966, Barbey has covered stories on every continent, and his work is regularly published in *Life*, the *Sunday Times* (London), *Stern*, *National Geographic*, *GEO* and *Paris-Match*. He is the winner of many prestigious awards and has exhibited his work in Paris, London, Rome and Zurich.

Nicole Bengiveno

San Francisco 1984

Nicole Bengiveno
American/San Francisco, California
Named Photographer of the Year in 1979 by the San Francisco Bay Area Press Photographers' Association, Bengiveno has been a staff photographer for the *San Francisco Examiner* since 1977. In 1983 she won first place in the Associated Press sports photo contest.

P.F. Bentley
American/San Francisco, California
Bentley is a *Time* magazine contract photographer. He recently completed 18 months' work covering the 1984 Presidential Campaign and for this work won first and second place in the U.S. Pictures of the Year competition.

Lucy Birmingham
American/Tokyo
Birmingham photographs for Gamma Press Images in Japan, as well as for numerous international publications. Her photographs have appeared on the cover of Japan Air Lines in-flight magazine, *Winds*. She says her love for Japan grows stronger the longer she lives there.

Torin Boyd
American/New York, New York
Boyd has worked as a news photographer for United Press International and the *Orlando Sentinel*. His pictures have appeared in *The New York Times*, *USA Today*, *Rocky Mountain News*, *Asahi Shimbun* and the *San Francisco Examiner*, among others. He is currently studying visual communications at Ohio University.

David Burnett
American/Washington, D.C.
A founding member of Contact Press Images, Burnett is the winner of many awards for photojournalism. He has covered such diverse subjects as the Iranian revolution, political developments in the Philippines, Korea, Portugal and Yugoslavia, Sadat's Egypt and Cambodian refugees in Thailand. His work has appeared on the covers of major news and feature magazines around the world. In 1980 he was named Photographer of the Year by the National Press Photographers Association and in 1985 he won the Olivier Rebbot Award from the Overseas Press Club.

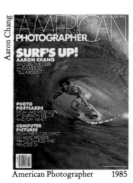

Aaron Chang

American Photographer 1985

Aaron Chang
American/Honolulu, Hawaii
Since 1979, Chang has been senior staff photographer for *Surfing* magazine. In 1982 he received the American Society of Magazine Photographers Award of Excellence and was named one of the five best sports photographers in the U.S. by *American Photographer*. His work has appeared in *Stern*, *American Photographer*, *Gentleman's Quarterly*, *French Vogue* and *People*. A cover story on Chang appeared in *American Photographer* while he was in Japan.

Gary Chapman

Florida 1978

Gary Chapman
American/Louisville, Kentucky
Chapman is currently a staff photographer for the Louisville *Courier-Journal Sunday Magazine*. His work has appeared in *National Geographic*, *Traveler*, *Time*, *Forbes* and *Newsweek*.

Paul Chesley
American/Aspen, Colorado
As a freelance photographer with the National Geographic Society since 1975, Chesley has traveled regularly to Europe and Asia. Solo exhibitions of his work have appeared at museums in London, Tokyo and New York. His work has also appeared in *Fortune*, *Time*, *Esquire*, *GEO* and *Stern*.

Rich Clarkson
American/Washington, D.C.
Clarkson is currently director of photography for *National Geographic* and a contributing photographer to *Sports Illustrated*. He has co-authored four books and his work has appeared in *Life*, *Time* and the *Saturday Evening Post*.

Jodi Cobb

A Day in the Life of Australia 1981

Jodi Cobb
American/Washington, D.C.
A staff photographer for *National Geographic* since 1977, Cobb has photographed major articles on China, Jerusalem, Jordan and London. In 1985 she was named the first woman White House Photographer of the Year. She holds a masters degree in photojournalism from the University of Missouri.

Jack Corn

Tennessee 1963

Jack Corn
American/Nashville, Tennessee
Corn is one of the senior figures in American news photography and has won many awards for photojournalism. His work has appeared in *Time*, *The New York Times*, *Life* and *The Philadelphia Inquirer*. He is currently director of photography at the *Chicago Tribune*.

Bob Davis
Australian/Hong Kong
Davis travels extensively on editorial, advertising and corporate assignments His black-and-white photos were featured in his book, *Faces of Japan*, and he is currently taking pictures for books on Tokyo and Macao. He is the owner and managing director of The Stock House, Asia's largest photo agency outside of Japan.

Greg Davis
American/Tokyo
Davis has been based in Tokyo for the past ten years and has worked all over Asia covering stories such as the assassination of Benito Aquino, the shooting down of Korean Airlines Flight 007 and the Bikini Islanders. His work has appeared in *Life*, *Time*, *Newsweek* and *National Geographic*. He won the Communication Arts Magazine Award for editorial photography in 1982.

Anne Day
American/New York, New York
Day has a particular interest in architecture, and she has published three books in W.W. Norton's Classical America Art and Architecture Series. Her work has also appeared in *Fortune*, *Newsweek*, *The New York Times*, *Avenue* and *Le Monde*.

Nicholas Devore
American/Aspen, Colorado
Prior to becoming a freelance
photographer, Devore was a
wilderness ranger and is still a
member of the Explorers Club.
In 1984, Devore photographed
the Cherry Blossom Festival in
Kyoto. His photographs have
been published in *National
Geographic, GEO* and other
international magazines.

A Day in the Life of Australia 1981

Arnaud de Wildenberg
French/Paris
A freelance photographer since
1984, de Wildenberg is best
known for his coverage of the
Afghanistan crisis and Iranian and
Cambodian refugees. He won the
Paris-Match contest for the best
news report in 1980 from
Uganda and an award from the
World Press Photo Foundation
for his coverage of Lech Walesa
of Poland. His photograph was
selected for the cover of *A Day in
the Life of Australia*.

Julio Donoso
Chilean/Paris
The recipient of a graduate degree
in economics from the University
of Paris, Donoso has photographed subjects ranging from
the New York City marathon to
Nicaraguan border towns to
students at the Harvard Business
School. He is a regular contributor to *Madame Figaro* and is associated with Contact Press
Images.

David Doubilet
American/New York, New York
Considered one of the world's
leading underwater photographers, Doubilet has been diving
since he was 13. He is a contract
photographer for *National
Geographic* which has published
over 20 of his underwater stories.
Winner of the SARA prize for
underwater photography,
Doubilet has dived in six of the
world's seven seas.

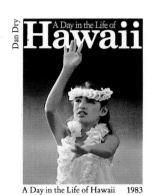

A Day in the Life of Hawaii 1983

Dan Dry
American/Louisville, Kentucky
Dry is a freelance photographer
for *National Geographic* and other
national and international
publications including *Time,
Newsweek, Town and Country* and
Sport. He has won over 300
awards and his newspaper work
was recognized by the National
Press Photographers Association
when he was named Newspaper
Photographer of the Year in 1981.
His photograph was selected for
the cover of *A Day in the Life of
Hawaii*.

Japan 1983

Tsuneo Enari
Japanese/Kanagawa
Enari worked as a photographer
for the Mainichi Shimbun in
Tokyo from 1962 to 1974 and has
worked in both New York and
Los Angeles. He has followed
post-war subjects such as Japanese
women married to American
military men and Japanese war
orphans abandoned in China.

Jennifer Erwitt
American/San Francisco, California
Erwitt served as production
director for *A Day in the Life of
Hawaii, A Day in the Life of
Canada* and *A Day in the Life
of Japan*. Her photographs have
appeared in all three books.
Erwitts' work has also been
featured in the New York Daily
News and Frets magazine. She is
the founding member of *Feline
Productions*.

New York 1978

Misha Erwitt
American/New York, New York
A native New Yorker, Erwitt has
been taking pictures since he was
11. After a long stint in the film
business, he took up editorial
photography and has been published in *American Photographer,
Esquire, People, Manhattan , Inc.*
and *USA Today*. He celebrated his
thirty-first birthday in Japan.

Victor Fisher
Canadian/Toronto, Ontario
Fisher served as logistical director
for *A Day in the Life of Japan*.
Following his photographic arts
studies at Ryerson Polytechnical
Institute he worked for
Masterfile, Canada's top stock
photography agency. Fisher's
work has appeared in *Interview*
magazine as well as in *A Day in
the Life of Canada*.

Masahisa Fukase
Japanese/Tokyo
A graduate of Nihon University,
Fukase worked for the Nihon
Design Center before becoming a
freelancer. In 1974, his photos
were selected for the Japanese
Photography Exhibition at the
Museum of Modern Art in New
York and in 1977 he won the
Nobuo Ina Award.

Rafael Gaillarde
French/Paris
Gaillarde is a Gamma news-
photographer. His in-depth
coverage of world events has appeared in many European magazines and his photo essay on the
Fallas festival in Valencia, Spain
appeared in *GEO*.

Wilbur E. Garrett
American/Washington, D.C.
The editor of *National Geographic,*
Garrett is also a working photog-
rapher who has won many
awards. Among his honors are
the Newhouse Citation from
Syracuse University, the Distin-
guished Service in Journalism
Award from the University of
Missouri and Overseas Press
Club and White House News
Photographers Awards for out-
standing photography. He holds
an honorary degree from the
University of Miami.

West Germany 1979

Diego Goldberg
Argentine/Buenos Aires
After beginning his photographic
career in Latin America as a correspondent for Camera Press,
Goldberg moved to Paris in 1977
as a Sygma Photos staff photographer and in 1980 moved to
New York. In 1985 he returned
to Argentina. His work has been
featured in the world's major
magazines and in 1984 he won a
World Press Photo Foundation
prize for feature photography.

Arthur Grace
American/Washington, D.C.
Grace's most recent work in-
cludes coverage of Pope John Paul
II's return to Poland, the 1983
World Cup races and a soon-to-
be-published book of personal
photographs. His photos have
appeared in *Time, Life, Look,
Newsweek,* the *Sunday Times*
(London), *Paris-Match* and *Bunte*.
Grace is associated with Sygma
Photos.

Tom Haley
American/Paris
A resident of Paris since 1974,
Haley won a 1982 University of
Missouri Photographic Award
for Feature Photography and a
1985 World Press Award for a
portrait series. He worked for
Magnum Photo Agency as a
researcher for three years in Paris
and New York and has worked
with Sipa Press since 1983.

Japan 1982

Hiroshi Hamaya
Japanese/Kanagawa
Hamaya is one of Japan's most
revered photographers. He began
his career in 1930. His work has
been exhibited internationally in
one-man and group shows.
Among his many books are *The
Document of Grief and Anger* and
Landscapes of Japan. In 1982,
Hamaya was awarded the
Shincho-sha Grand Prix Award
for Fine Arts. He sees the major
focus of his work as man and his
environment.

Al Harvey
*Canadian/Vancouver, British
Columbia*
After being voted ''Least Likely
to Succeed,'' Harvey left school
to see the world. Without
photographic training, but with
an Instamatic as his companion,
he stumbled into shooting for
audio-visual productions. His
present clients include several
Canadian a/v production houses,
airlines, resource and manufac-
turing companies and government departments.

National Geographic 1983

David Alan Harvey
American/Richmond, Virginia
Harvey's assignments for *Na-
tional Geographic* in the past 12
years have included Kampuchea,
Honduras, Grenada, Mayan
ruins, Spain and the Arctic. In
1978, Harvey was named
Magazine Photographer of the
Year by the National Press
Photographers Association.

Jyoji Hashiguchi
Japanese/Saitama
Hashiguchi studied at the Aoyama School of Photography and has been a freelance photographer since 1975. He has published three books and is working on a project focusing on zoos in the great cities of the world. In 1981, he received the Taiyo Award.

Gregory Heisler
A Day in the Life of Australia   1981

Gregory Heisler
American/New York, New York
Heisler has contributed covers and cover stories to *Life, Fortune, Time, Esquire, Connoisseur, Money, Business Week* and *The New York Times Magazine* and has photographed for corporate publications and advertising. He produced the last two performance books of the American Ballet Theatre and intends to do more fashion photography in the future.

Ethan Hoffman
Life magazine   1980

Ethan Hoffman
American/New York, New York
Hoffman is an internationally recognized photojournalist who has recently completed photo essays in Japan for *Life, Fortune, The New York Times Magazine* and *Connoisseur.* His work has appeared in major magazines around the world and Time-Life Books is publishing a book of his work on Japan. He is president of Archive Photos.

Cliff Hollenbeck
American/Seattle, Washington
Hollenbeck specializes in travel and advertising photography and was named Travel Photographer of the Year in 1983. He has worked for major magazines, airlines and travel organizations and produces the television series "Journeys."

Eikoh Hosoe
Japanese/Tokyo
Winner of many awards for photography and internationally recognized for his photographs of Hiroshima, Hosoe is Professor of Photography at the Tokyo Institute of Polytechnics. He has exhibited all over the world and his work is part of many museum collections. His books include *Ordeal by Roses, Man and Woman* and *Kamaitachi.*

Takeji Iwamiya
Japanese/Hyogo
A professor at the Osaka University of Arts since 1966, Iwamiya has photographed throughout Asia. The winner of the Mainichi Arts Award and the Ministry of Education Award for Selective Arts, his books include *The World of the Japanese Garden* and *Imperial Gardens of Japan.*

Adam Jahiel
American/Los Angeles, California
With a degree from the University of Missouri School of Journalism, Jahiel has focused on editorial and industrial photography. His pictures have appeared in the *Kansas City Star* and *The New York Times.* For two years he assisted Douglas Kirkland in Hollywood, and has since freelanced for Sygma Photos.

Lynn Johnson
American/Pittsburgh, Pennsylvania
As a contract photographer for Black Star since 1982, Johnson has shot for *Life, Newsweek, Forbes* and *Fortune.* Earlier she spent seven years as a staff photographer for the Pittsburgh Press during which time she won seven Golden Quill Awards. In 1985 she received a World Press Award and a Robert F. Kennedy World Understanding Award.

Pauline Johnson
Canadian/Toronto, Ontario
A freelance photographer and writer, Johnson frequently works for *The Toronto Star, Canada Post,* Canadian Cultural Newswire and publications in England and the United States. She was the associate director of photography for *A Day in the Life of Canada.*

Katsumi Kasahara
Japanese/Tokyo
A graduate of Hosei University, Kasahara has been a freelance photographer and has worked with Associated Press since 1977. In 1985 he won a News Photo Award from the New York Deadline Club.

Shelly Katz
American/Dallas, Texas
Raised in New York, Katz sold his first pictures to the *New York Daily News* when he was 12 years of age. A *Time* contract photographer, Katz has lived in Dallas since 1965. Since then his assignments have ranged from the space program to presidential campaigns to Brooke Shields. He is represented by the Black Star agency.

Kent Kobersteen
American/Washington, D.C.
Before joining *National Geographic* as an illustrations editor in 1983, Kobersteen spent 16 years as a staff photographer at the *Minneapolis Tribune* and two years editing the *Tribune's* Sunday magazine. Assignments have taken him to over 20 countries, primarily throughout Africa, the Middle East and Asia. He has won numerous awards including the 1981 Overseas Press Club Award for Newspaper and Wire Service Photography, special recognition in the 1982 World Understanding competition and the 1982 World Hunger Media Award for Photography.

Koo Bohn-Chang
Korean/Seoul
In 1975 Koo received a degree in Business Administration from Yon-Sei University in Seoul and in 1985 he received a diploma in Communication and Photo Design from the Fachhochschule Hamburg. He is a foreign correspondent of the Deutsche Gesellschaft für Fotografie and has exhibited his work in Korea and Germany.

Masanori Kobayashi
Japanese/Osaka
The 1982 first-place winner in the Yomiuri Photo Contest for news photography, Kobayashi has photographed extensively in the Third World. He has traveled to over 55 countries, covering issues such as hunger, discrimination and refugees for United Nations magazines.

Steve Krongard
American/New York, New York
Krongard's work ranges from the real to the fantastic, both on location and in the studio. His editorial work has appeared in most major magazines, and his advertising and corporate clients include American Express, IBM, Kodak, Shell, Dunhill and many others.

Hiroji Kubota
Burma   1978

Hiroji Kubota
Japanese/Tokyo
In 1970, Kubota received the first Kodansha Publishing Culture Award given by Japan's largest publishing house. He has produced many articles on Asia for the world's press and in 1981 was selected as the Japanese Photographer of the Year. Kubota's extensive work in Burma and China has resulted in a series of award-winning books.

Kaku Kurita
Japanese/Chiba
Kurita is one of Japan's most successful international photographers. His work has appeared in *Time, Fortune, Newsweek, The New York Times, Forbes, Paris-Match, Figaro, Le Point, L'Express* and *Stern.* He has worked for Gamma Press Images in Tokyo for ten years.

Shisei Kuwabara
Japanese/Tokyo
A graduate of Tokyo Agricultur[al] University and Tokyo College o[f] Photography, Kuwabara has bee[n] a freelance photographer since 1960, covering such diverse subjects as Minamata, Korea and Vietnam. His most recent book [is] about Korean pottery.

J.P. Laffont
India   19[]

J.P. Laffont
French/New York, New York
Laffont attended the prestigious School of Graphic Arts in Vevey Switzerland prior to serving in the French Army in Algeria in the early 1960s. He has served as the New York correspondent for Reporters Associates and Gamm[a] Press Images. Since 1973, he has been a partner of the Sygma Photo Agency based in New York. His work appears regularl[y] in the world's leading news magazines.

Andy Levin
American/New York, New York
Levin is a talented photographer well known for his shots of New York. He is published regularly i[n] *New York* magazine and in *Signature,* for whom he has traveled the world. In 1985 he won first prize in the National Press Photographers Association Pictures of the Year competition for a story on the Statue of Liberty. He is associated with the Black Star agency.

Ian Lloyd
Canadian/Singapore
Lloyd lives and works in Singapore producing books and videos on travel-related subjects. He has recently completed books on Bangkok, Hong Kong and Singapore, as well as two books on architecture and one on aerial photography. His work also appears in magazines such as *Time, Newsweek, GEO* and *Fortune.*

Saudi Arabia   1976

...erd Ludwig
...erman/New York, New York
...founding member of the
...isum Photo Agency in Ham-
...urg, Ludwig is a regular con-
...ibutor to *GEO, Life, Zeit
...agazin, Stern, Fortune* and other
...agazines. He is a member of
...eutsche Gesellschaft für
...otografie (the German Photo-
...raphic Society) and the Art
...irectors Club of Germany.
...nce 1984 he has worked out of
...ew York.

...eonard Lueras
...merican/Honolulu, Hawaii
...ueras is the editorial director of
...mphasis International, an Asia-
...ased book and magazine pub-
...shing group. He specializes in
...e Pacific and Asia and since
...978 has written, edited and pro-
...uced 14 books about culture and
...avel in the region. His most re-
...nt book is *Surfing, The Ultimate
...easure* and he is presently work-
...g on a book about Bali.

...rtugal   1972

...y Maisel
...merican/New York, New York
...ne of the most sought-after
...hotographers in the world,
...aisel's work appears regularly
... magazines, advertisements and
...orporate publications. His color
...rints are included in numerous
...orporate and private collections.
...e received the Outstanding
...chievement in Photography
...ward from the American Soci-
...ty of Magazine Photographers in
...978 and the Newhouse Citation
...om Syracuse University in
...979.

Hiroyuki Matsumoto
Japanese/New York, New York
A graduate of Chiba University,
Matsumoto has lived in New
York since 1973. He is associated
with the Black Star agency and
his work appears in *National
Geographic, GEO, Newsweek* and
other international magazines.

Toshiyuki Matsumoto
Japanese/Tokyo
A film major at Paris University
from 1974–75, Matsumoto has
been a freelance photographer
since 1978. He has photographed
political events for *Time, Newsweek, Life, Paris-Match* and
Fortune.

Stephanie Maze
American/Washington, D.C.
Born in New York and raised
in Germany, Maze was a staff
photographer for the *San Francisco Chronicle* for six years. Since
1980 she has been a freelance
photographer working primarily
with *National Geographic* covering Mexico, Puerto Rico, Cata-
lonia and Brazil.

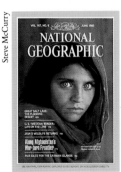

National Geographic   1985

Steve McCurry
American/New York, New York
A freelance photographer for
National Geographic, McCurry
won the 1980 Robert Capa Gold
Medal Award for his work in
Afghanistan and the 1984
Photographer of the Year Award
from the National Press
Photographers Association. He
has won four first-place awards in
the World Press Photo Contest in
Holland and is associated with
Magnum Photos.

Jun Miki
Japanese/Tokyo
A graduate of Keio University,
Miki has worked for Sun News
Photos and Time-Life. Since 1957
he has been a freelance photogra-
pher and has won many awards.
He is a professor at Nihon
University and has been president
of the Japan Photographic Society
since 1981.

India   1984

Dilip Mehta
Indian/Toronto, Ontario
Mehta is an internationally recog-
nized photographer associated
with Contact Press Images. In
1985 he won two World Press
Awards and a special citation
from the Overseas Press Founda-
tion for his coverage of the
Bhopal, India industrial tragedy.
His work has appeared in *Time,
GEO, The New York Times, Paris-
Match, Newsweek, Bunte, Le
Figaro* and *Fortune.*

Rudi Meisel
German/Hamburg
Meisel is a founding member of
Visum, one of West Germany's
top photo agencies. Since 1975
his work has appeared in *Zeit
Magazin, Art, Der Speigel, Stern*
and *GEO.* He has won numerous
awards. He is currently working
on a photo project entitled, "The
Industrial Heart of Germany:
The Ruhr District."

Michael Melford
American/New York, New York
Along with his work for corporate and industrial clients,
Melford was a regular contributor to *GEO* and won several
awards for a cover story on "The
Kodo Drummers of Japan." He
has also received prizes from
Communication Arts, Art Direction,
the World Press Photo Foundation and the Missouri School of
Journalism.

Maddy Miller
American/New York, New York
Currently assistant photo editor
of *People,* Miller has worked at
Look and *Us* and has freelanced
for many major magazines. She
has also worked as a photographer for MADRE, an organization involved with the women
and children of Nicaragua.

Masaaki Miyazawa
Japanese/Tokyo
Awarded the first International
Center of Photography Young
Photographer Award in 1985,
Miyazawa is a graduate of Nihon
University. His series "Dream in
Ten Nights" has been exhibited
twice in Tokyo.

Kazuyoshi Miyoshi
Japanese/Tokyo
Among his many awards,
Miyoshi has received the Adver-
tising Photographers' Associa-
tion Grand Prize in 1979 and the
Japan Photographic Society Silver
Award in 1980. His book *Paradise*
was published in 1985.

Robin Moyer
American/Hong Kong
Moyer's coverage of the conflict
in Lebanon was recognized with
two prestigious awards in 1983:
the Press Photo of the Year
Award in the World Press Photo
competition and the Robert Capa
Gold Medal Citation from the
Overseas Press Club of America.
A *Time* contract photographer,
he is associated with Gamma-
Liaison.

Beirut   1983

James Nachtwey
American/New York, New York
A Black Star photographer since
1980, Nachtwey has covered
world conflict in Northern
Ireland, Lebanon and Central
America. In 1984 and 1985 he
won Overseas Press Club Robert
Capa Gold Medal Awards and in
1983 was named Magazine
Photographer of the Year in the
National Press Photographers
Association Pictures of the Year
competition.

Japan   1984

Yoshiaki Nagashima
Japanese/Osaka
A graduate of the Japan College
of Photography, Nagashima has
been a freelance photographer
since 1963. His 1984 book *One
World, One People* received the
Award of Excellence for book
design from *Communication Arts*
magazine.

Masatoshi Naito
Japanese/Tokyo
A 1961 graduate of Waseda
University and the recipient of
many awards, Naito has pub-
lished four books since 1979. His
photos were selected for the New
Japanese Photography Exhibition
in 1974 at the Museum of
Modern Art in New York.

Ikko Narahara
Japanese/Tokyo
Narahara lived and worked in
Europe and New York after
graduating from Chuo University. In 1956 he held his first one-
man exhibition in Tokyo and
marks this as the beginning of his
career as a photographer. Since
then he has had numerous exhibitions in Japan, the U.S., Canada
and Europe.

A Day in the Life of Hawaii   1983

Matthew Naythons
American/San Francisco, California
A working photojournalist and
physician, Naythons has spent
most of his career alternating between photo coverage of world
events and emergency room duty
in San Francisco. In 1979 he
founded an emergency medical
team to care for Cambodian and
Thai refugees. His photographic
work appears regularly in major
magazines.

Kazuyoshi Nomachi

Sudan   1980

Kazuyoshi Nomachi
Japanese/Tokyo
Nomachi began freelancing in 1971 and since then has made several trips to North Africa and the Sinai resulting in the books *Sahara* and *Sinai* published in five languages. He has also published books on the Nile and a second book on the Sahara which won Japan's Ken Domon Prize.

Graeme Outerbridge
Bermudan/Hamilton
Named the 1985 Young Outstanding Person of the Year in Bermuda, Outerbridge has exhibited his work in New York, Washington, D.C., London, Boston and Helsinki. He has published *Bermuda Abstracts* and is currently working on a book about bridges.

Bill Pierce

New York   1974

Bill Pierce
American/New York, New York
A *Time* magazine contract photographer associated with Sygma, Pierce has won the Overseas Press Club's Olivier Rebbot Award for Best Photo Reporting from Abroad for his work in Belfast, Beirut and Cairo. He was educated at Princeton University.

Jon Pite
American/New York, New York
A corporate and advertising photographer, Pite has been widely exhibited in North America and Europe. His editorial work has appeared in *Connoisseur, The New York Times, Ambiente* and *Architectural Digest.*

Eli Reed
American/New York, New York
Reed is a veteran of the Middletown, New York *Times Herald Record* and the *Detroit News.* For the *San Francisco Chronicle* he covered urban poverty and the conflicts in Lebanon and Central America. In 1982 he was awarded the prestigious Nieman Fellowship at Harvard University. Reed is working on a book about the condition of blacks in North America 20 years after the civil rights movement. He is associated with Magnum Photos.

Alon Reininger
Israeli/New York, New York
Upheavals in Nicaragua and El Salvador, developments in Honduras, the AIDS epidemic, the development of the Cruise and Pershing II missiles, the Papal visit to Peru and cocaine smuggling in Florida are among Reininger's stories for the world's leading magazines. He is a founding member of Contact Press Images.

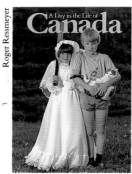

Roger Ressmeyer

A Day in the Life of Canada   1984

Roger Ressmeyer
American/San Francisco, California
A 1975 graduate of Yale University, Ressmeyer is a freelancer whose work has appeared in *Time, People, Fortune, Newsweek, Life* and *Science Digest.* His specialties include portraiture, fashion and high technology. He founded the Starlight Photo Agency. His photograph was selected for the cover of *A Day in the Life of Canada.*

Galen Rowell
American/Berkeley, California
Rowell is one of the world's outstanding environmental photojournalists. His work has appeared in *National Geographic, Outside, Audubon, Sierra* and *Sports Illustrated,* and he has traveled widely throughout the U.S., Asia, Africa and the South Pacific in the course of his assignments.

Bill Simpkins
Canadian/Calgary, Alberta
Simpkins worked for the *Calgary Herald* for 14 years and is now employed in the public affairs department of Petro-Canada. His work has appeared in several magazines, and he has published a book on Alberta. He is the winner of a Canadian Press Award.

Tom Skudra
Canadian/Toronto, Ontario
Since 1967 Skudra has worked for a variety of clients in Canada and abroad, including the Canadian government, *Maclean's, Quest, The Globe and Mail* and Labatt's Breweries. He is a three-time winner of the Toronto Art Directors Club Award for Photojournalism.

Neal Slavin
American/New York, New York
The recipient of numerous awards, Slavin is published regularly in the *Sunday Times* (London), Stern, GEO, Town & Country, Newsweek and *Connoisseur.* His work has appeared in one-man and group shows and he has just completed his third book, *Britons.*

Rick Smolan

South Korea   1981

Rick Smolan
American/New York, New York
Co-director of the *A Day in the Life of Japan* project, Smolan is also responsible for *A Day in the Life of Australia* (1981), *A Day in the Life of Hawaii* (1984) and *A Day in the Life of Canada* (1984). Prior to these extravaganzas, Smolan was a full-time photojournalist whose work appeared in major publications such as *Time* and *National Geographic.*

Andrew Stawicki
Canadian/Toronto, Ontario
After working as a staff photographer in Frankfurt for *Bild Zeitung* and in Warsaw for *Swiatowid,* Stawicki joined *The Toronto Star* in 1983. He has won several prizes in Poland and Holland and has exhibited his work in Poland and in Canada.

Issei Suda
Japanese/Tokyo
A graduate of the Tokyo College of Photography, Suda spend three years as a staff photographer for the experimental theater Tenjo Sajiki. A freelance photographer since 1971, he has contributed to various camera magazines in Japan and has published a book about Tokyo.

Kiyomi Takeyama
Japanese/Tokyo
The recipient of a degree in photography, Takeyama is currently photographing Japanese *buto* dancers and has been traveling with the Byako-sha troupe.

Junichi Tanabe
Japanese/Yokohama
Tanabe describes himself as a self-taught photographer who has been a freelancer since 1963. In 1985, he published a book on aging, a subject which has been of special interest to him since 1965.

Shomei Tomatsu
Japanese/Tokyo
For two years Tomatsu worked for Iwanami Photographic Books and he has been a freelance photographer since 1956. Since then he has also taught photography at the Tokyo University of Art and Design and received many awards for his work. He specializes in themes related to post-war situations in Nagasaki and Okinawa.

Neal Ulevich

Thailand   1977

Neal Ulevich
American/Beijing
Ulevich is the Associated Press photographer and photo editor for China. He has spent 16 years photographing news events in Asia and has lived in Japan, Thailand, South Vietnam and Hong Kong. His photos of violent political upheaval in Bangkok won the 1977 Pulitzer Prize for news photography.

Mark S. Wexler
American/New York, New York
Wexler travels the world as a photographer for a variety of editorial and corporate clients including *Time, Life, Smithsonian* and *Stern* He has produced several major photo essays for *Fortune,* the most recent a portfolio on luxury cruise liners.

Joy Wolf

Arizona   1985

Joy Wolf
American/Tucson, Arizona
Wolf's major subjects have included prostitutes in Nevada, relocated Navajo Indians and the U.S.–Mexico border. Her work is in the collection of the Center for Creative Photography and has been published in the *San Jose Mercury News, The Palm Beach Post and Evening Times* and the *Arizona Daily Star* where she worked as a staff photographer.

Haruyoshi Yamaguchi
Japanese/Tokyo
A 1970 graduate of the Chiyoda School of Photography, Yamaguchi has worked for United Press International and is represented by Gamma Press Images. In 1975 he won second place in the UPI Photo Contest.

Munesuke Yamamoto
Japanese/Tokyo
Yamamoto works for Pacific Press Service in Tokyo. His work has appeared in *Japan Graphic,* and he has assisted major Japanese and visiting international photographers.

Mike Yamashita
American/Mendham, New Jersey
Yamashita spends a good deal of his time in the Far East photographing for *National Geographic* and for corporate clients such as Nikon, Singapore Airlines and Diners Club. His book *Lakes, Peaks and Prairies: Discovering the U.S.–Canadian Border* was published in 1984.

Staff Members

Produced and Directed by:
Rick Smolan and David Cohen

Managing Editor
Spencer Reiss
Newsweek Magazine

Art Director
Leslie Smolan
Carbone Smolan Associates

Written by:
Murray Sayle

Translator and Writer, Japanese Edition
Ken Tajima

Honorary Director
Hiroshi Hamaya

Publicity Director
Patti Richards

Publicity Consultant
Daiji Kobayashi
International Public Relations Co., Ltd.

Production Director
Jennifer Erwitt

Logistics Director
Victor Fisher

Associate Production Director
Torin Boyd

Production Assistants (Tokyo)
Andy Morey
Joanne Scherrer
Eric Weyenberg

Production Assistants (New York)
Jay Kennedy
Elizabeth Pisani

Senior Assignment Editor
Arnold Drapkin
Time Magazine

Assignment Editors
Greg Davis
Anne Day
Neil Gross, *Time-Life News Service*
Pauline Johnson, *The Toronto Star*
Yuko Katsumura
Jenny Sayle
Yutaka Suzuki, *Pacific Press Service*
Kiyomi Takeyama
Munesuke Yamamoto

Consulting Editor
Jane Condon
People Magazine

Special Assignment Editor
Koko Kato

Controller
Ellen Bailey

Legal Advisor
F. Richard Pappas
Paul, Weiss, Rifkind, Wharton & Garrison

Financial Advisor
Richard Levick

Picture Editors
Woodfin Camp
Woodfin Camp & Associates
Mary Dunn
People Magazine
John Durniak
U.S. News & World Report
Sandra Eisert
San Jose Mercury News
Kent Kobersteen
National Geographic
Yukiko Lanois
Black Star
Brent Peterson
Parade Magazine
Leslie Smolan
Carbone Smolan Associates
Tsuguo Tada
Iwanami Publishing

Film Traffic Director
Anne Romer
World Press Photo Foundation

Symposium Coordinators
Robert Kirschenbaum
Akira Kijima
Pacific Press Service

Debriefing
Deviyani Kamdar

Broadcast Rights Consultants
Sandy Smolan
Gilles St. Marie

Editorial and Research Coordinator
Rita D. Jacobs, Ph.D.

Researchers
Kitty Harmon
Yuko Katsumura

Assistant Art Director
Thomas K. Walker
Carbone Smolan Associates

Designers
Ann Harakawa
Diane LeMasters
Robin Williams

Project Logo Design
Lori Barra

Collins Publishers
Ian Chapman
Chairman
George Craig
Vice-Chairman
Alewyn Birch
Group Managing Director–International
Nicholas Harris
President, Collins North America
Sonia Land
Group Finance Director
Janice Whitford
Editorial Director, Collins North America
Mary Adachi
Grace Deutsch
Copy Editors
Bill Conner
Int'l Marketing Manager, Collins North America

Toppan Printing Co., Ltd.
Tetsuro Minami
Project General Manager, Japan
Shinichi Sugiura
Project Manager, Japan
Yuji Utsumi
Project Assistant Manager, Japan
Mitsuhiro Tada
General Manager, New York
Mickey Endo
Sales Manager, New York

Agents

Canada
Steve Pigeon
Chris Moseley
Mike Fisher
Masterfile, Stock Photo Library
2 Carlton Street, #617
Toronto, M5B 1J3
Phone (416) 977-7267
In Vancouver (604) 734 2723

France
Annie Boulat, Cosmos
56 Boulevard de la Tour
   Maubourg
75007 Paris
Phone 705 4429, Telex 203085

Germany
Marita Kankowski, Focus
Schlueterstrasse 6
2000 Hamburg 13
Phone 44 3769, Telex 2164242

Hong Kong
The Stock House
310 Yue Yuet Lai Bldg
43-55 Wyndham Street
Hong Kong
Phone 5 220486 or 5 224073
Telex 78018

Italy
Grazia Neri
Via Parini, 9
20121 Milano
Tel 650832 or 650381
Telex 312575

Japan
Bob Kirschenbaum
Pacific Press
CPO 2051, Tokyo
Phone 264 3821, Telex 26206

United Kingdom
Terry Le Goubin
Colorific Photo Library
Gilray House, Gloucester
   Terrace, London W2
Phone (01) 723 5031 or 402 9595

United States
Woodfin Camp & Associates
415 Madison Avenue
New York, NY 10017
Phone (212) 750 1020
Telex 428788

Sponsors, Advisors, Contributors and Consultants

Sponsors

Underwriter
American Express International
Incorporated

Major Sponsors
Kodak Japan K.K.
Japan Airlines
Tokyo Hilton International
Apple Computer Inc.
Olympus Cameras

Major Contributors
Far East Laboratories
Foreign Press Center, Japan
Horiuchi Color Lab
International Christian University
Japan External Trade Organization
(JETRO)
Ken Lieberman Laboratories
Nagase Sangyo
NHK (Japan Broadcasting
Corporation)
Nissan Automobile Corporation
Pacific Press Service
Petro-Canada
Philip Morris Asia Inc.
Shashin Kosha Laboratory
Time-Life News Service, Tokyo
Bureau

Contributors

Aero Asahi Corporation
All Nippon Association for the
Welfare of the Aged
Arts & Communication
Counselors
Asahi Culture Center
Associated Press
Big Western Restaurants
Black Star Publishing Co., Inc.
Cathay Pacific Airlines
Chase Manhattan Bank
Chunichi Dragons Baseball Team
Comet Corporation
Contact Press Images
Coopers & Lybrand
Cross Cultural Exchange Center
of Osaka
Daisho Corporation
Defense Agency, Japan
Do Sports Plaza
Emphasis International
Enryakuji Monastery
Esquire Magazine
Federal Express Corporation
Fieldings Guides

Foreign Correspondents Club of
Japan
Fujita Wan-Nyan Association
Office
Gamma-Liaison
General Assoc. of Korean
Residents in Japan
General Videotex Corporation
Ground Self Defense Force,
Women's Training Unit
Hanbara Elementary School,
Aikawa-cho
Hibuna Kindergarten, Kushiro
Hiroshima Peace Museum
Hokkaido Dairy Farmers Co-
operative
Hokkaido Kushiro Hokuyo
Senior High School
Hokkaido Prefectural Office,
Kushiro Branch
Hokkaido University
Ibusuki Iwasaki Hotel
Ikeda High School
Image Photographic Services
Imperial Palace Outer Park
Administration Office
International Public Relations
Co., Ltd.
Ito City Tourist Association
Iuppa/McCartan Inc.
Iwasaki Holdings Company
Japan National Tourist
Organization
Japan Pictorial Quarterly
Japanese National Railways
Japanese Self Defence Agency
Jiyu Gakuen School
Jujin Hospital
Kabukiza
Kanamachi Fire Department
Kobe Steel
Kokusai Air Company
Kokusai Kagaku Gijyutsu
Hakurankai Kyokai
Kokusai Kanko Shashin
Company Ltd.
Komaya Ryokan
Kushiro City Hall
Kushiro Zoo
Kyoto Movie Village
Living Videotex Corporation
Macworld Magazine
Magnum Photo Agency
Maritime Safety Agency
Maritime Self Defense Force
Officers Candidate School
Maryknoll Mission, Sanya
Matsumoto-shi Kinro Shinshosha
Okunai Pool
Ministry of Foreign Affairs
Mitsukoshi Department Store,
Nihonbashi
Mudoji Buddhist Monastery
Nagoya International Center

Namerikawa Harumi Teichi
Fishing Cooperative
National Geographic Society
National Puppet Theater
New York Filmworks
Newsweek Magazine, Tokyo
Bureau
Nissho Iwai Corporation
Osaka Police Headquarters
Otaru City Canal Preservation
Society
Parade Magazine
Paul, Weiss, Rifkind, Wharton
& Garrison
People Magazine
Photographic Society of Japan
Police Agency Administration
Rishiri Oshidomari Fishermen's
Cooperative
San Jose Mercury News
Seiko Watch Company Limited
Shibamata Gakuen
Shikoku Seinoh Trucking
Company
Shinjuku Sumitomo Building
Sunakku Rei
Society to Introduce Kanazawa to
the World
Sony Corporation
Stanford Alumni Association
Stryker Weiner Associates
Surfing Life Magazine
Sushi University of Japan
Suzuki Violin Association
Sygma Photos
Taisho University
TDK Corporation
Teito Rapid Transit Authority
Teshikaga Town Office
The Chicago Tribune
The Tokyo Stock Exchange
The Weekender
Time Magazine
Tobio Kindergarten
Tohoku University
Tokyo Disneyland
Tokyo Fire Agency
Toppan Printing Company Ltd.
Toyama Prefecture Office
Toyo Kanzai Co. Ltd.
Tsukuba Exposition 1985
Tuttle-Mori Agency
United Nations University
Visuals International Publications
Ltd.
Woodfin Camp Associates
World Press Foundation
Yoshida Kogyo Company Ltd.
Yokohama Customs
Yomiuri Shimbun Newspapers
Yonaguni Island City Office
Zen Corporation

Friends, Advisors and Consultants

Kozo Abe
Mal Adams
Guy R. Aelvoet
Masahiro Aida
Toshiharu Akiba
Corky Alexander
William E. Allison
Ryuichi Anashige
Arata Ando
Wyatt Andrews
Hajime Aoki
The Aoki Family
Matthew Aoyagi
Toshiro Arai
Shigeyoshi Araki
Takeshi Araki
Makoto Asagoe
The Asagoe Family
Kiyoshi Asano
Wakaba Asaumi
Herbert Asherman
Toshiro Ashiki
Takeji Ashizawa
Mari Awata
Yoshiko Awazu
Yoshiaki Bannai
David Bell
Gussie Bergerman
David P. Biehn
Smoke Blanchard
Susan Bloom
Jim Boff
Del Borer
Frances J. Bragdon
Wendy Brennan
Richard V. Bryant
Robert Burns
Ken Carbone
Chris Carey
Ian Chapman
Tom Chapman
Sadeo Chida
Judy Ann Christensen
Albert Chu
Rhoda & Jesse Claman
Daniel Cohen
Gail Cohen
Hannah Cohen
Jerry Cohen
Norman Cohen
Rose Cohen
Shura Cohen
James Colligan
Robert J. Collins
Bill Connor
Robert Cory
George Craig
Hanneke Cruz
Tracey Dahlby
Robyn Davidson
Raymond H. DeMoulin
Liz Detwiler
Sheila Donnelly
Larry Doyle
Gayle Driskell
Gene Driskell
Natasha Driskell
Harumi Ebihara
The Ebihara Family
Keiko Ebuchi

Michiko Egawa
Kaoru Endo
Kyoko Endo
Mickey Endo
Keiko Enya
Jeff & Sue Epstein
Elliott Erwitt
Ellen Erwitt
John Espey
Sgt. Ed Evans
Corinne Ferguson
William A. Feuillan
Sinwa Findegarten
James A. Firestone
Kosai Fujii
Reiko Fujii
Tokuyoshi Fujii
The Fujii Family
Jun Fujisawa
Masako Fujita
Michiko Fujita
Kazu Fujiwara
Masakuni Fujiwara
Yasuhisa Fujiwara
Toshiharu Fukita
Kazuhiko Fukuda
Yoshiaki Fukuda
Koichi Fukushima
Seiji Furuta
Toshinori Fuyutsume
Harris Gaffin
Nanette Geller
Masahiro Goda
Kenkichi Goso
Bill Grimm
Bin Haga
Hidenobu Hagiwara
Itsuko Hamada
Hiroshi Hamaguchi
Muneo Hanaue
Richard E. Handl
Jun Hani
Judy Hansen
Miyo Harie
Nicholas Harris
Sakae Haruki
Taizo Haruna
Trish Harwood
S. Hasegawa
Kozo Hashimoto
Norio Hashimoto
Juinichi Hattori
Junko Hattori
Takehiko Hayakawa
Masatoshi Hayase
Goi Hayashi
Misao Hayashi
Rie Hayashi
Tsuneo Hayashida
August Hergesheimer
Bill Hersey
James Higa
Ryo Higashino
Eiichi Hiradate
Masao Hirata
Naoki Hirayama
Hachiro Hirose
Hideaki Hirose
Isao Hirowatari
Thonong Hirunsi
Susan Hoene
Madoka Hori
Hiroko Horie

Minoru Horiuchi	Jyo Koshida	Masanori Nagase	Itaru Saito	Mikiko Tanaka
Yukio Hosaka	Virginia Kouyoumdjian	Masahiro Nagata	Katsuhisa Saito	Minoru Tanaka
Hidetoshi Ichihashi	Ken Krugler	Motohiko Nakada	Minoru Saito	Kengo Tanako
Takeshi Ichinosawa	Akiko Kuga	Susumu Nakada	Mitsuko Saito	Atsushi Tange
Rev. Masao Ichishima	Takao Kuga	Evelyn Nakagawa	Takeo Saito	Hiroyuki Tasaka
Hiroyuki Iida	Tazuko Kuma	Rev. Masamitsu Nakagawa	Tetsusaburo Saito	Kazuo Terashima
Tatsuhiko Iida	Sumiko Kurita	Yoshihiro Nakai	Yo Saito	Umekichi Terashima
Osamu Iijima	Norio Kurita	Jun Nakajima	Junko Sakakibara	Uki Terukuni
Toshiko Ikawa	Hiroko Kuroda	Satoshi Nakajima	J. Curtis Sanburn	Mary Testa
Gyoun Imadegawa	Yukiko Kuroda	Hideo Nakamura	Kai Sanburn	Yuriko Tezuka
Shoichi Imai	Toshio Kurosaki	Hiroshi Nakamura	Koji Sasaki	Tetsuo Tokunaga
Maki Inoue	Tsutomu Kurosawa	Myoshin Nakamura	Shigeaki Sasaki	Yoichi Tomisawa
Satoko Inoue	Seiji Kusaka	Y. Nakamura	Kio Sato	Tatsuhisa Torii
Yachiyo Inoue	Eliane Laffont	Yoshio Nakamura	Yasuaki Sato	Tsuyako Toyonaga
Tsutomu Ishibashi	Sonia Land	Takemi Nakanishi	Yoshiharu Satoh	David Tracey
Mari Ishii	Larry A. Leochner	Atsuko Nakano	Sada Sazuki	Terry Trucko
Kazuhiro Ishijima	Martin Levin	Toshio Nakano	Fred Scherrer	Akio Tsuboi
Hiroshi Ishikawa	David Lewis	Sharon Nakazato	Carolyn See	Koichi Tsuchida
Keiko Ishikawa	Li Bang Li	Nick Nishida	Hiromoto Seki	Kenichiro Tsuchiya
Noriaki Ishimatsu	Ken Lieberman	Hiroko Nishikawa	Takako Seki	Kiyokazu Tsuda
Prof. Takafumi Isomura	Curt Ludwigson	Kana Nishimuta	Chieko Sekikawa	Reiko Tsujimura
Erika Itami	Bruce MacDonald	Tetsusaburo Nishito	Tsuyoshi Shibayama	Rita Tsukahira
Sachio Itami	Haruyuki Machida	Kazuyoshi Nishizawa	Manabu Shigeta	Geoffrey Tudor
Vern Iuppa	Shooji Machida	Professor Nishizawa	Atsuo Shimada	Hajime Uchikoshi
Masayoshi Iwaki	Isozo Maeda	Sharon Nivison	Kikuko Shimazaki	Nobuo Ueda
Yutaka Iwakiri	Nobuaki Maeda	Mihoko Nobumasa	Takamasa Shimizu	Itaru Uehara
Hideo Iwase	Koichi Maefusato	Hideaki Nohara	Yoko Shimizu	Fumimichi Ujiie
Maggie Jackson	Yoshihisa Maitani	Yuichi Nomura	Nobuo Shimose	Haruji Ukai
Richard S. Jiloty	Mineo Makado	Miyoshi Norihiro	Kiyomi Shinozaki	Terukini Uki
Geraldine Johnson	Asako Makino	Kenjiro Oe	Shokin Shinzato	Masanari Umakoshi
Jennifer Josselson	Tadashi Makino	Junko Ogawa	Shunzo Shirai	Hisashi Umebara
Kunio Kadowaki	Yuji Makino	Kaoru Ogimi	Mitsuro Shiraishi	Yoshiyuki Umeoka
Shinji Kagami	Kaori Makita	Kenichiro Ohe	Sueo Shirasawa	Yasuharu Umezu
Hirotsune Kageyama	Alfred Mandell	Akiko Ohkubo	Bun Shoh Liu	Hoichi Urata
Nina Kaiden Wright	Capt. Steve Manuel	K. Ohtani	Tohru Shukuya	Tomonobu Uryu
Tahao Kajiwara	Mike Marshall	Kazumi Ohtsuka	Albert L. Sieg	Takaya Usutani
Kenji Kakuta	Mary Ann Maskery	Seichi Ohya	Morris Simoncelli	Shunsho Utsumi
Nobuyuki Kano	Ayumi Matsubara	Shigemitsu Ohzahata	Gloria Smolan	Della Van Heyst
G. Karasawa	Hiroshi Matsubara	Haruo Ohzu	Marvin Smolan	Haruyuki Wada
Ed Kashi	Sonoko Matsuda	Yukio Oike	Taepyong So	Shogo Wakabayashi
Akira Kashiwagi	Hiroki Matsumoto	Katsumi Oka	Shinsaku Sogo	Hiroko Watabe
Shugi Kasuya	Masaka Matsumoto	Toshio Okada	Jim Stockton	Masahiro "Frank" Watanabe
Mutsumi Katayama	Akiko Matsunaga	Issei Okajima	Lynne Strugnell	Nori Watanabe
Makoto Kato	Tatsuo Matsuoka	Akiyoshi Okamoto	Masayuki Sueda	Tokusuke Watanabe
Tetsuya Kawabe	Shisho Matsushima	Dr. Rokozou Okamoto	Shoji Sugai	Shinji Watarai
M. Kawada	Suzanne Matsushima	Eiichi Okamoto	Akinori Sugimura	Tadashi Watarai
Moriyoshi Kawagoe	Hidefumi Matsutaka	Haruhiko Okazaki	Kyoko Sugimura	Matthew N. Winokur
Jane Kawamoto	Tsuyoshi Matsuyama	Toko Okazaki	S. Sugiura	David Wong
Yoshitaka Kawamoto	Gary Matteoni	Kazuhiko Okishio	Peter Sutch	Simon Worrin
Kinji Kawamura	Lucienne Matthews	Yoshiaki Okuizumi	Nancy Suttles	Joyce Wouters
Ken Kawasaki	Richard Matthews	Kenji Onishi	Hidefumi Suzuki	Yoshio Yamada
Alex Kerr	Ruth McCreery	Hiroyuki Onuki	Shinobu Suzuki	Keiji Yamaguchi
Masahiro Kihara	Mineo Mikado	Kazuko Onuki	Mitsuhiro Tada	Ryuichi Yamanaka
Akiko Kikuzawa	Toshiya Mikuni	Shigeko Onuki	Akiyasu Tajima	Michiko Yamaoka
Itaru Kikuzawa	Nascia Miller	Ned Oshiro	Maseo Takabatake	Komyo Yamatoda
Tom Sok Kim	Ted Minami	Toshiaki Ozaki	Rie Takahama	Seseko Yamazato
Miko S. Kim	Machiko Minegishi	Yasuyuki Ozu	Hidehiko Takahashi	Kiyoshi Yamazoto
A. Kimura	Ida Mintz	Nicholas Palevsky	Ikuo Takahashi	Takayuki Yanada
Maya Kimura	Takeya Mitani	Dan Parkenham	Toshiki Takahashi	Miho Yanagida
Mokunen Kimura	Norihiro Miyoshi	Anne Pepper	Masao Takahata	Takiji Yanagisawa
Yoshio Kimura	Phillip Moffitt	Elizabeth Perle	The Takamasa Shimizu Family	Ken'ichi Yazawa
June Kinoshita	Shinichi Momose	Gabriel Perle	Kosuke Takaoka	Takao Yoneda
Tetsuo Kitamura	Toshiaki Morinaga	Robert Pledge	Asami Takasawa	Raymond Yonke
Yohei Kobayashi	Akio Morita	Elizabeth Pope	Yuji Takeda	Megumi Yoshii
Tsutomu Kobayashi	Tetsuaki Morita	David Powell	Yutaka Takeda	Masakazu Yoshizaki
Yutaka Kobayashi	Takeo Moriya	Richard Pyle	Yuko Takemoto	Tomiko Yoshizawa
Mr. & Mrs. Kiyoharu Kodama	Toru Moriya	Edwin Reingold	Masato Takenaka	Wakako Yuki
Yoshikazu Kohda	Masuo Morodomi	Jim Reston Jr.	Hiro Takeuchi	
Chikara Kojima	Kimiko Morohashi	Kearney Rietman	Jun Takita	
Nayuki Kokubo	Kevin Moss	Volkmar Ruebel	Toru Tamaoki	
Yasuhiro Komatsubara	Koichi Murakami	Tom Ryder	Nobuo Tamura	
Akiyuki Konishi	Takashi Nagaoka	Kan Sagara	Norio Tanabe	
Yohei Kono	Toshio Nagasaka	Hideo Sagawa	Hiroyuki Tanaka	

Thank you to the People of Japan